Computerized Manufacturing and Human Resources

Issues in Organization and Management Series
Arthur P. Brief and Benjamin Schneider, *Editors*

Employee Ownership in America: The Equity Solution
Corey Rosen, Katherine J. Klein, and Karen M. Young

Generalizing from Laboratory to Field Settings
Research Findings from Industrial-Organizational Psychology, Organizational Behavior, and Human Resource Management
Edwin A. Locke, editor

Working Together to Get Things Done
Managing for Organizational Productivity
Dean Tjosvold

Self-esteem at Work
Research, Theory, and Practice
Joel Brockner

Implementing Routine and Radical Innovations
A Comparative Study
Walter Nord and Sharon Tucker

The Outsiders
Jews and Corporate America
Abraham Korman

Organizational Citizenship Behavior
The Good Soldier Syndrome
Dennis W. Organ

Facilitating Work Effectiveness
F. David Schoorman and Benjamin Schneider, editors

Futures of Organizations
Innovating to Adapt Strategy and Human Resources to Rapid Technological Change
Jerald Hage, editor

The Lessons of Experience
How Successful Executives Develop on the Job
Morgan W. McCall, Jr., Michael A. Lombardo, and Ann M. Morrison

Computerized Manufacturing and Human Resources
Innovation through Employee Involvement
Roy B. Helfgott

Computerized Manufacturing and Human Resources

Innovation through Employee Involvement

Roy B. Helfgott
New Jersey Institute of Technology

Lexington Books
D.C. Heath and Company/Lexington, Massachusetts/Toronto

Library of Congress Cataloging-in-Publication Data

Helfgott, Roy B.
  Computerized manufacturing and human resources.

  Includes index.
  1. Labor supply—United States—Effect of technological innovations on. 2. Computer integrated manufacturing systems—Economic aspects—United States. 3. Industrial management—United States—Employee participation. I. Title.
  HD6331.2.U5H45 1988   331.25   87–46380
  ISBN 0–669–18029–7 (alk. paper)

Copyright © 1988 by Industrial Relations Counselors, Inc.

All rights reserved. No part of this publication may be reproduced or transmitted in any form or by any means, electronic or mechanical, including photocopy, recording, or any information storage or retrieval system, without permission in writing from the publisher.

Published simultaneously in Canada
Printed in the United States of America
International Standard Book Number: 0–669–18029–7
Library of Congress Catalog Card Number 87–46380

The paper used in this publication meets the minimum requirements of American National Standard for Information Sciences—Permanence of Paper for Printed Library Materials, ANSI Z39.48–1984. ∞™

88 89 90 91 92 8 7 6 5 4 3 2 1

Contents

Figures and Tables ix

Foreword and Acknowledgments xi
Richard A. Beaumont

Introduction xv

1. **Computer-based Technologies** 1

    Computer-aided Design 1
    Industrial Robots 2
    Numerically Controlled Machine Tools 3
    Automated Materials-handling Systems 4
    Automated Storage and Retrieval Systems 5
    Vision Systems 5
    Computer-controlled Systems 6
    Implementation of Programmable Automation 6

2. **Planning the Introduction of New Technology** 9

    Role of Employee Relations 9
    Employee Involvement 13
    Conclusion 16

3. **Communications** 17

    Company Communication Efforts 17
    Forms of Communication 18
    Creating a New Industrial Relations Climate 19
    Failure to Communicate Adequately 21
    Collective Bargaining Requirements 21

4. **Reactions to New Technology**   25

5. **Training and Retraining**   31
   - Need for Training   31
   - Matching Jobs and Workers   33
   - Training throughout the Organization   34
   - Designing Training Programs   38
   - Thoughts on Training   42

6. **The Employment Effects of Computer-based Technology**   43
   - Complexity of Problems Besetting Industry   43
   - Positive Role of Innovation   47
   - Cases of Employment Increase   48
   - Impact on Women, Minorities, and Young Workers   49
   - Changed Composition of the Labor Force   50
   - Short-Term Employment Outlook   54

7. **Dealing with Displacement**   57
   - Attrition   57
   - Temporary Employees   59
   - Early Retirement   60
   - Intraplant Transfers   62
   - Interplant Transfers   63
   - Employee Reassignment   65
   - Benefits for Displaced Workers   65

8. **The Nature of Jobs and the Organization of Work**   67
   - The Changing Nature of Jobs   67
   - Deskilling and Upskilling   70
   - Broadening Jobs   72
   - The Work Environment   74
   - Problem Areas   76

9. **Employee Involvement**   79
   - Development of Employee Involvement   79
   - Union Attitudes toward Employee Involvement   81
   - Management Attitudes toward Employee Involvement   83
   - Technology and Involvement   84
   - Contrasting Views   86
   - Sociotechnical Approaches   86
   - Training for Sociotechnical Systems   88

10. **Organization and Management Structure** 93

    Plant Departmental Organization 93
    New Ways of Managing 95
    Open Organization 97

11. **Union Responses** 101

    Labor-Management Conflict 103
    Seniority 104
    Job Classifications 107
    Bargaining Unit Work 109
    Compensation 111
    Economic Security 113
    Employee Involvement 116
    Nonunion Labor Relations 119
    Conclusions 121

12. **Implications for the Future** 125

    Conclusions from the Study 125
    Living with Technological Change 129
    Cushioning the Impact of Change 132
    Marching into the Future 133

Appendix A: Robotics Study Sponsoring Companies 137

Appendix B: IRC Study of the Impact of Robotics on Human Resources and Employee Relations 139

Notes 161

Index 167

About the Author 173

Figures and Tables

Figures

9–1. Organization Chart of Cable Plant Using Sociotechnical Approach to Work Organization   92

10–1. Continuum of Organizational Design Strategies   99

Tables

2–1. Employee Attitudes, before and after Introduction of New Technology   16

6–1. Employment Changes in Electronic Instrument Plant, before and after Introduction of New Technology   51

6–2. Employment Changes in Electrical Products Plant, before and after Introduction of New Technology   52

6–3. Distribution of Employment within the Bargaining Unit, by Job Grade, Division Manufacturing Electronic Control Device for Aircraft   53

6–4. Change in Distribution of Employment in Plant Unit Converted to a Flexible Manufacturing System   53

Foreword and Acknowledgments

A fundamental goal of Industrial Relations Counselors, Inc. (IRC) since its founding in 1926 as the first industrial relations research organization is to advance the knowledge and practice of human relationships in the workplace. To that end, IRC has undertaken pioneering studies in such areas as paid vacations, industrial pension systems, unemployment insurance, and equal employment opportunity.

A particular concern over time has been seeking ways to introduce technological innovation with minimum adverse effects on people. Two decades ago, IRC studied the impact of hard automation.[1] In 1984 it decided to examine the impact of programmable automation technology. The study, "The Impact of Computer-based Technology on Human Resources and Employee Relations," was conducted with the financial support of the Alfred P. Sloan Foundation and a number of leading companies. Representatives of those companies constituted an advisory committee for the study.

The IRC study was conducted in two phases. The first was a survey of business and labor leaders and experts in the field of automation to ascertain their opinions regarding the new technology. The survey was conducted in the United States, and then replicated in the United Kingdom through the cooperation of the Institute of Personnel Management. The survey questionnaire and the responses are summarized in Appendix B.

The second phase of the study was empirical research on actual company experience in planning for and implementing new computer-based technology. This book is a report of its findings. The research team visited sixteen companies and one or more of their automated facilities. (Of these companies, one refused to let us visit a production facility, but it did discuss its policies and programs for dealing with new technology.) The facilities visited were geographically dispersed, from New York to California, from South Carolina to Minnesota. Many different manufacturing industries were involved: aircraft, automobile, chemical, communications equipment, computer, electrical, instruments, machinery, shipbuilding, and steel. With one exception, the companies visited were either themselves large or subsidiaries of large companies. A typical visit spanned two days—one at headquarters and one at a facility. In some cases, where facility and headquarters were in the same location, the visit was shortened to one day, and in other cases three or more days were spent with a company.

The plants visited were at various stages in the introduction of the new technology examined: in planning, in the process of implementation, and in operation. Because technological innovation is an ongoing process, in many plants visited, programmable automation of one type had already been implemented in one operation, and a different application was in process of introduction in another operation. As a result, the companies cannot usefully be classified according to stages of introduction of new technology.

One idea advanced within the advisory committee of companies supporting the study was to compare the levels of technological advancement in computer-integrated manufacturing among the various companies. This too proved to be impossible because of the varieties of technologies in use. There is no one way to determine, for example, whether a state-of-the-art computerized continuous casting process in one industry is more or less advanced than a flexible manufacturing center in another.

As originally conceived, the IRC study was to be on the impact of robotics. At the first meeting of the advisory committee, it became apparent that limiting the study's scope to robots would miss some of the most important technological advances. For the purposes of this study, robotics has been defined to include all forms of programmable automation (that is, as equivalent to computer-integrated manufacturing), and the new technology includes robots, numerically controlled (NC) machine tools, and automated materials-handling, storage, and retrieval systems.

A second problem that had to be dealt with concerned the scope of the study. Again in consultation with the advisory committee from industry, IRC decided to study only the manufacturing plant itself and not to examine automation in central offices or self-contained warehouses. The study thus focuses on manufacturing in the plant, from the delivery of raw materials at the loading dock to the shipment of finished goods out the gate.

We observed a great variety of computer-based technologies. In most cases, we saw islands of automation—an NC machine with a robot arm or an advanced computerized numerically controlled (CNC) machining center capable of performing forty-six different operations or a robot performing materials-handling functions. Several companies are tying together such islands to create flexible manufacturing centers or even computer-integrated manufacturing. Another technology observed was that of automatic materials-handling and/or storage and retrieval systems. In transportation equipment, robots are being used for a variety of tasks, such as spray painting and welding. In metals industries, automated continuous casting processes were seen. A synthetics plant visited was actually a conglomeration of computerized production and control systems. Indeed, computer-controlled manufacturing processes were a major type of programmable automation encountered.

The introduction of new technology to increase productivity, reduce production costs, improve product quality and reliability, and through its greater flexibility make possible rapid response to market shifts is essential if American manufacturing is to regain its competitive position. New technology has been a major contributor to the recent resurgence in U.S. manufacturing productivity. Resistance to technological innovation—whether in the form of union pressure, government regulations, or employee apprehension—could seriously hamper management efforts to put the new technology speedily into operation and gain its benefits.

Recognizing the importance of advanced technology to the future of American manufacturing, IRC undertook this study to ascertain the human resource impacts of new computer-based technology and to determine the best ways of dealing with them while gaining the most from the new technology. By finding out what actions companies have taken in the past and what is likely to happen in American manufacturing in the future, we hope to provide policy guidance with respect to the introduction of new technology. Through the provision of information, it may be possible to forestall resistance to the new technology. Understanding the interaction of people and technology, moreover, can point to directions in which companies should be moving.

On behalf of Industrial Relations Counselors, Inc., I want to express my appreciation to those who have made this study possible. The financial support provided by the Alfred P. Sloan Foundation and a number of leading companies was essential to the conduct of the study and, we hope, was put to good use. IRC is particularly indebted to Albert Rees, executive director of the Sloan Foundation, for his recognition of the importance of the topic of human adjustment to technological change. The many people in the case study companies, from production workers on the shop floor to vice-presidents, deserve special acknowledgment for the time they gave the research team and the information they so willingly supplied. Any misinterpretation of the source material, however, is the responsibility of IRC.

A number of people associated with IRC played vital roles in the research effort. The major credit goes to Roy B. Helfgott, distinguished professor of economics at the New Jersey Institute of Technology, for directing the study and writing this book. Dr. Helfgott was assisted by David Kuperschmidt and Deborah Seidman; Ms. Seidman had major responsibility for processing the opinion survey. For the replication of the opinion survey in the United Kingdom, IRC acknowledges the support of the London office of Organization Resources Counselors, Inc. and the Institute of Personnel Management, with special thanks to Theon Wilkinson of the IPM. Charles

A. Tasso, president of IRC, has been a source of advice and wisdom. I especially want to thank Denise Rathbun, who has so meticulously edited the manuscript.

We trust that many people, particularly those working toward the achievement of a more prosperous manufacturing sector through the integration of human and technological elements, will find the book of help to their efforts.

Richard A. Beaumont
IRC Director of Research

Introduction

The idea of progress, which has dominated Western thought for centuries,[1] was carried to new heights with the emergence of industrialization in the eighteenth century as humans learned to harness the forces of nature to achieve material prosperity. Economic growth promised continued advancement and ever-higher living standards.

Effects of Technological Progress

Economists' traditional conception of industrial expansion was largely one of increased investment and the continued substitution of capital for labor. In recent years, some economists, Nathan Rosenberg in particular, have asserted that technological innovation is the true source of economic growth.[2] Indeed the 1987 Nobel Prize in economic science was awarded to Robert Solow for his pioneering work in quantifying the contributions of capital stock increases and innovation to economic growth.[3] Rosenberg defines technological progress as "any improvement in the relationship between inputs and outputs." New technology—new methods of production, products, organization systems—alters the production function (the combination of labor and capital), providing more output from a given amount of labor and capital, thus permitting economic growth and rising living standards.

Industrialism and technology, however, have also had negative impacts—most conspicuously the disruption of people's lives and the spoliation of the environment.[4] Technological innovation in particular has continually aroused fear and resistance among those whose livelihood was threatened by it, since the Luddites smashed the new textile machinery in the early nineteenth century. This was the initial reaction to hard automation in the 1960s as exemplified by AFL-CIO president George Meany's likening it to "a curse to this society."[5]

Problems Besetting U.S. Manufacturing

Although technological innovation has become an accepted part of our lives, it has not lost the capacity to instill fear that millions of workers will be displaced from their jobs. This concern about the consequences of technological change now comes at a time when a large portion of U.S. manufacturing is struggling to solve severe economic problems.

A domestic economy has been replaced by one that is complex and worldwide, in which the United States is no longer the dominant force. All advanced nations have expanded their economies, and new countries have joined the ranks of the industrialized. With the slowing of world economic growth, many industries are experiencing global overcapacity. Furthermore, many American industries are saddled with plant that is old and obsolete. As a result, not only have markets abroad been lost, but imports have taken large shares of domestic markets, with a concomitant loss of jobs for American workers. Some loss of markets was inevitable as increased technological diffusion allowed the less-developed nations, formerly confined to labor-intensive products, to compete in the production of technologically more advanced ones, as for example, electronics and now the Hyundai from Korea. American manufacturing, however, also has lost ground to other highly industrialized nations.

Decreasing competitiveness stems from factors ranging from product design and inferior quality to poor marketing, but the prices of American goods have also been a cause. Even before the value of the U.S. dollar shot up, American production costs were well above those of other countries, particularly Japan. Usually the high wages of American workers are blamed, but more important has been insufficient growth in productivity, that is, output per unit of input.

From 1973 to 1979, output per man-hour in the U.S. manufacturing sector rose at a rate of only 1.4 percent per year compared with 3.2 percent per year from 1960 to 1973.[6] In this same period, moreover, a number of other industrial nations were recording much higher productivity growth. During the past two and one-half decades manufacturing productivity in the United States grew at a rate that was just half that of eleven other industrial nations. The productivity problem is highlighted by the motor vehicle and equipment industry, in which output per employee hour more than doubled from 1957 to 1977 but declined 3.5 percent to 1981.[7] Wages meanwhile were going up, and quite rapidly, with the result that U.S. labor costs became considerably higher than those of competitors.

Some people view these developments as part of a process of maturation in which the United States will specialize in providing services while other nations make products. No nation, however, can support a large service sector without a strong manufacturing base. For reasons of both national defense and economic welfare—these industries provide employment for millions—manufacturing competitiveness must be restored.

Introduction of New Technology

How is manufacturing competitiveness to be regained? Clearly lowering wages is not an answer; American wages cannot be brought down to the levels prevailing in Korea, Taiwan, and other rising competitors. Instead manufacturers must introduce new computer-based technology, better utilize the human input to the production process, and develop and implement new ways of managing and structuring organizations. This approach is beginning to succeed, as evidenced by the recent resurgence in U.S. manufacturing productivity.

Recognizing the importance of advanced technologies to the future of American manufacturing, Industrial Relations Counselors undertook a study to ascertain their human resource and employee relations impacts, with the goal of determining the best means of dealing with those impacts while gaining the most from the new technology. This book is the report of the study's findings. It focuses on manufacturing; nevertheless, there are human resource imperatives in introducing technological change in any economic sector. Before we examine them, however, let us briefly define the new technology.

Computer-based technology includes the following:

Computer-aided design, whereby the drafter or design engineer generates the desired lines and shapes on a video screen by typing at a computer keyboard.

Robots, which according to the Robot Institute of America are "reprogrammable multifunctional manipulators designed to move material, parts, or specialized devices, through variable programmed motions for the performance of a variety of tasks."

Numerically controlled (NC) machine tools that shape or cut metal according to programmed instructions.

Automated materials-handling systems, which are the physical link joining workstations in a computer-based manufacturing environment.

Automated storage and retrieval systems, which are computer-based warehouses.

Vision systems, which rely on a combination of optical instruments and computers to perform such tasks as quality control and machine guidance.

Various forms of computer-controlled systems, such as automated continuous casting processes.

Flexible manufacturing systems combine workstations. They operate under central computer control. When the programmable automation ties together design, manufacturing, and management in an integrated system, computer-integrated manufacturing (CIM) is the result. Nobody has yet achieved true CIM, largely because of software problems—the various pieces of the system are unable to communicate with each other—but the technological problems will be overcome in time.

Many benefits flow from the utilization of computer-based technology. The first is increased productivity accompanied by reduced production costs. Another is improved product reliability; the accuracy of the work of a human being varies over the course of a day, but a programmed machine tool will repeat the same operation with flawless and tireless accuracy. Greater reliability also may mean reduced numbers of inspections and less material waste. Time also is a crucial factor. Computer-aided design and manufacturing make it possible to manufacture a prototype in one week rather than the seven to eight weeks required in the past. Similarly, at a plant visited, the greatest benefit of an NC machine tool with a robot arm for loading was not the savings in labor costs but a reduction in setup time. When a different-sized bearing had to be machined, setup was reduced from an average of thirty hours on the old automatic screw machines to one-half hour of reprogramming.

Computer-based technology makes the workplace safer and healthier because robots take over the most hazardous jobs. The greatest long-run benefit of this technology, however, is the flexibility it provides to respond quickly to market shifts. It enables batch (low-volume) production, which is characteristic of most U.S. manufacturing today, to achieve some of the advantages common to continuous process and mass production systems. Given the decline in product life cycles, it will enable all manufacturing to move from one product to another quickly as demand for a particular item drops, and making for more stable employment as well as higher company profits.

Human Resource Imperatives

If the new technology is to be introduced and used successfully, the human resource function must be involved at every stage of planning and implementation. There are clear human resource imperatives in introducing new technology: plan, communicate, train, deal with displacement, change the structure of work, and where organized, handle the union response.

Plan

The complexity and scope of the changes brought about by the new technology, along with its capital requirements, necessitate extensive planning to determine how, when, and where it will be introduced into the manufacturing system, as well as how it will be implemented. Because innovation such as the introduction of just-in-time inventory systems often forces changes in other modes of operation, its impact on organizational design also must be foreseen. Appropriate planning is essential to ease the transition from old to new systems.

Introducing computer-based technology thus poses new challenges to the human resource function. Human resource planning should be an integral part of a company's program for the introduction of technological change. Intensive efforts are required to prevent disruptions within the existing work force while retraining employees for the demands of the new technology. Technological change also presents new opportunities for the employee relations function: to change the way work is organized, involve employees in pursuit of enterprise goals, and reverse the traditional adversarial labor-management relationship.

Communicate

Communications and advance notice are vital to the planning process for technological change. The introduction of new technology, like any other innovation in the workplace, induces anxiety among employees. Concerns about job security, ability to handle new or altered jobs, and work group integrity arise, and they tend to provoke resistance to change. An employer seeking to secure the cooperation of its work force and where organized, the union, must assuage fears about the impact of the technology on jobs and work life.

An important finding of our study is that there has been an almost total absence of resistance to new technology. Indeed, the resistance that has been manifested has been greater in middle and lower management ranks than among rank-and-file workers. Unions too have not sought to block or hamper management's implementation of the new technology.

That there has been so little resistance to new technology is due in large part to companies' communications efforts. An effective communications program starts by explaining in detail the need for technological change in terms of strengthened company competitiveness. Advance notice of impending change must include information on its nature, the effects it will have on employees, and the ways in which the company plans to aid those who might be adversely affected. Companies should consider not only informing employees but allowing those who are to operate the new technology to play a role in the planning process.

Train

The key to successful implementation of computer-based technology is training. Companies should regard their work forces as valuable assets that are renewable through retraining in new skills. By investing in training, a company ensures that it will have a work force capable of efficiently operating new processes.

Failure to train employees adequately can lead to problems that undermine efficient operations. Poorly trained workers make mistakes that result in parts rejects and the need for costly rework. Moreover, under automation, with its integration of production, worker errors can lead to system breakdowns and even to serious accidents.

Insufficient attention to training often leads to unanticipated problems, as experienced by one plant that introduced an entirely new process for manufacturing its product. Preparation for the change took place when plant employment was down, and only the existing work force was retrained. Management did not anticipate the speed and vigor of the resurgence in sales and found itself operating a second shift before it could get additional retraining underway. The original training had been conducted largely by the vendors, but the contractual training provisions had expired, forcing plant management into crash programs. The cost of that training, moreover, had to come out of operating budgets.

Some hard lessons emerge from this experience. First, management must carefully determine training needs, estimate their costs, and then build in those costs to project budgets. Otherwise funds necessary for adequate instruction may not be available. Before training costs can be estimated, however, human resources must work closely with engineering and manufacturing to identify the jobs for which people will be retrained and the skills needed in those jobs. Delineating new skill requirements, however, is not easy because the jobs must be analyzed while the technology is under development and not yet clearly understood. This, of course, is why interaction of human resources with design and manufacturing is so important.

Another lesson that emerges is that, to the degree possible, companies should engage in in-house training rather than place too much reliance on vendors. Finding trainers within the organization may not be easy if this is a first venture into computerized manufacturing, but relying on equipment vendors has its drawbacks too. Vendor-provided training often is superficial; vendors are unfamiliar with the facility's culture and may encounter human relations problems; and vendors will not be responsible for future training.

Managers also should make sure that training is replicable so that as additional workers are needed, they can receive proper instruction in operating and controlling new equipment. Management should be imaginative and utilize new training techniques, including the computer itself. Employees who use computer training modules can study on their own and get immediate feedback. Also it is neither wise nor necessary to rely solely on professional trainers, for employees can learn from one another. Indeed peer training is particularly effective.

Plants moving toward greater employee involvement and autonomy will find that specific training in this work approach is essential, especially for supervisors who must become team leaders rather than production pushers. One general mistake companies have made is to neglect training of salaried personnel. Supervisory training is of paramount importance, particularly because many foremen tend to be deficient in technical areas. Training is called for at all levels, including managerial and professional employees. Many engineers, out of school for a decade or more, know virtually nothing about computer-based technology. Some companies are sending them back to school for course work in the new technologies.

Management cooperation with the local educational community can further this objective. Universities can provide general education and human relations training while the company provides training on specific technology. Many companies have concluded that the presence of a university is a requisite in the location of new plants.

Finally, the programmable automation revolution is continuous; training therefore cannot be a one-time effort. On the contrary, training must be continuous, and the skills of the work force must be constantly upgraded to match the requirements of continually advancing technology.

Deal with Displacement

A major hypothesis with which IRC began its study, which was substantiated by the findings, is that the new technology will not have devastating effects on companies' work forces; although the nature of the technology is revolutionary, implementation is being accomplished in an evolutionary manner. Since the new technology has been introduced gradually, and for a variety of reasons—technical, economic, and managerial—its further implementation will continue to be so, companies are afforded the time in which to plan to avoid large-scale employee displacement.

Although programmable automation does not necessarily create additional jobs, the greater efficiency and flexibility that accompany it should allow manufacturing industries to become more competitive and thus regain market shares that have been lost. Gains in sales and production, however, are not always equal to the increase in efficiency, so there may be a decline in total employment at a plant. Consequently, management must establish programs to ease this impact.

A reduction in human resource requirements need not lead to employee displacements. Allowing normal attrition to trim the work force before new technology is introduced is the most helpful way of minimizing separations of employees. Careful human resource planning is necessary if work force reductions are to be accomplished through attrition. If attrition is to be sufficient to avoid layoffs, companies must be careful not to inflate their work forces by new hiring prior to the introduction of new technology. Among the techniques that can be used are more efficient utilization of the current work force, overtime work that can be eliminated as personnel requirements decline, hiring of nonpermanent workers, and internal transfers and retraining.

The use of temporary employees during transition periods to new technology, when both the old and the new processes must be operated simultaneously, is sensible, as attested to by the experience of one high-tech communications equipment plant that was introducing a flexible manufacturing system in one department. While the regular work force was being retrained, a large group of workers was required to operate the old process and to aid in debugging the new. A temporary hiring service provided the plant with 455 workers at the peak of the transition. The strategy proved to be a success. It enabled plant management to accomplish its goal of introducing the new technology without personnel shortages and without first hiring and then having to lay off hundreds of employees, which would have been damaging to employee morale. The plant's human resource department, moreover, could not have handled such a massive recruitment effort in such a short period. The temporary agency did all the screening, training, and paperwork.

Attrition often can be speeded up by making early retirement financially attractive for older workers. Early retirement may have a high financial cost, but many companies prefer it to laying off younger workers, who have young families and hence greater financial needs, who are the company's future work force, and who often are more amenable to retraining and thus work more effectively with new technology.

Effecting transfers in order to prevent loss of employment is another principal element in human resources planning. Smoothly effecting transfers, however, depends on astute human resource management, since almost all facets of employee relations are involved, from training to seniority practices. Most transfers caused by new technology are rather simple, with a worker being moved from one job to another within the same department. In some cases, the entire department may be affected, so the employees must be transferred within the plant.

In transferring displaced workers, management should seek to provide them not only with alternative jobs but also with jobs that are comparable in compensation to their old ones. Retraining becomes the means by which workers can qualify for similarly rated positions. If jobs with comparable pay are not available, the alternative is to maintain workers at previous higher rates of pay ("red circle" rates). One must be careful, however, not to use red circle rates on a widespread basis for that tends to undermine a plant's wage structure. According to the experience of a computer manufacturer that extends rate protection to workers displaced by technology, about three years of normal attrition are needed to work out red circle rates so that a plant's wage structure is once again in line with its job evaluation system.

A few companies transfer workers to other facilities when there are no opportunities at the home plant. This practice is more common with companies that have a number of plants in a given labor market area and workers can be shifted without relocation. Although interplant transfers of blue-collar workers are not usual, it is customary to give preference to those laid off at one plant in hiring at another.

Sometimes fortuitous events may make interplant transfers possible. One company faced a sharp cutback in personnel requirements, due in part to new technology, at a plant of one of its divisions. At the same time, another division was experiencing product demand growth and sought company investment funds for expansion of one of its plants. Since the two plants were within an acceptable commuting distance, corporate headquarters, under the prodding of the human resource function, made release of funds to the expanding division contingent on its acceptance of the workers displaced at the plant of the other division. As a result, no employees lost jobs.

In situations in which employees do lose their jobs, companies can provide severance pay, supplementary unemployment benefits, income continuance, job placement aid, and/or education and retraining assistance.

Change the Structure of Work

The revolutionary nature of computer-based technology is most evident in its effects on the structure of manufacturing operations, the work environment, the nature of jobs, and the ways in which work is organized. Unless companies institute the required organizational changes, they will not reap the optimum benefits of advanced technology.

The traditional system of work organization, in which jobs are arranged in a hierarchy of distinct, often multiple classifications, each assigned a separate wage rate, no longer fits manufacturing needs. There must be greater flexibility in the utilization of the work force. Rigid demarcations must give way to more multiskilled jobs, and compensation systems must be revised to reward workers for broadening their knowledge bases. Hourly employees should be given greater control over their work and more authority in performing it. Furthermore, with the introduction of the computer, information, formerly a monopoly of managers, may become available to workers on the shop floor, enabling them to act on their own.

Strenuous, repetitive, hazardous work is being eliminated, while requirements of responsibility, knowledge, and willingness to exert authority are increasing. Workers have to do less but think more; analytical skills come into play. Where formerly they operated machines, they now monitor and are responsible for expensive equipment. The discretionary parts of jobs increase. Employees must diagnose problems in order to prevent system interruptions, which are extremely costly under automation.

One company is using a new venture as a laboratory in which to try out new ideas. Traditional job classifications have been modified, and production workers are helping to determine how the work is done. Teamwork is the key to the new work organization. In an assembly operation, an individual who believes something is wrong can stop the line, and this is having a tremendously positive impact on morale and also yielding a high-quality product. Another work organization innovation is that in which setup formerly carried out by industrial engineering staff is now being done by the hourly employees—and more efficiently. Overall there has been a sharp increase in output per worker.

Authoritarian control of the work force is passing from the scene. A management system that put all decision making in the hands of superiors not only destroyed worker motivation but also denied employers the benefit of the ideas that workers could have contributed to improve production methods. American management is being converted to a belief in employee involvement. Although computer-based technologies can increase productivity, product reliability, and workplace safety, they must still be operated by people. Consequently companies are discovering that people are equally important to the accomplishment of organizational objectives.

The introduction of new technology can be combined with a recognition of the importance of the human contribution. Line managers, as well as employee relations specialists, have called attention to the fact that workers on the plant floor are often well educated and have tremendous potential for growth. Workers' familiarity with operations means that they have much to contribute to improved efficiency. The typical approach is to have regular meetings of the work group and its supervisor, known as quality circles, to report on progress and to discuss production problems and devise solutions to them.

Companies trying employee involvement are pleased with the results to date. By being involved in the planning and implementation of new processes, employees become receptive to them and the changes required of themselves. Involvement in problem solving has led to many suggestions of ways to achieve greater efficiency.

Not everyone, whether within management, unions, or academia, approves of employee involvement. Shaiken and his associates claim that worker participation programs are part of an "ideology of competition" promoted by management to make workers believe that greater efficiency and job security are connected.[8] Employee involvement efforts thus "encourage workers to adopt a managerial perspective when production problems arise on the shop floor and to gain personal satisfaction from contributing ideas that promote efficiency." Although Shaiken may decry this, in view of the need for cooperative effort to restore manufacturing competitiveness, by which jobs can be sustained, this statement becomes one of the best arguments for employee involvement ever advanced. It clearly is the best means by which management can gain employee commitment to organizational goals.

In a few cases, employee involvement has gone well beyond the quality circle, to the application of sociotechnical systems theory. The major features of this new way of organizing work are worker autonomy in carrying out assignments; flexibility in job assignments, with each worker capable of and actually performing different tasks, with pay according to knowledge; and teamwork, with group interaction and commitment. An important element of such an organization of work is feedback to the group.

The examples of the application of sociotechnical work organization include one in which it has been operating successfully for a decade, a clear indication that positive achievements were not simply a Hawthorne effect, a result of the novelty of the situation. This approach to the organization of work has had a tremendous impact on the organizational structure in these plants, particularly in the elimination of layers of management. Since the teams assume most of the functions assigned to foremen in traditional plants, the managers' concerns are facilitating the teams' needs.

The reaction of managers and production workers to this way of organizing work is positive. A plant manager with twenty-five years of experience in traditional operations, stated, "I always knew that there had to be a better way of running a plant, and now I've found it." One of the workers on the floor reported, "I like this setup because there is no boss breathing down my neck and no union restricting what I can do."

The way in which industrial organizations are managed also is changing. The typical seat-of-the-pants decision making by managers is giving way to planning decisions based on the information provided by the system. Not surprisingly, middle managers and foremen feel threatened as they see the "little black books," through which they had exercised control over operations, being made obsolete. These individual collections of notes and procedures gained from years of experience were their personal data bases, and abandoning their informal systems is difficult for many of them. Managers must learn not merely to work a little differently but to conceptualize an entirely new way of operating and managing an integrated people-process system. Instead of acting as watchdogs and disciplinarians, they must become planners, trainers, and communicators.[9]

A revolution in the organization of industrial enterprises is afoot. Layers of management are being stripped away, decision making is being pushed down the scalar chain, and work is being redesigned to be more meaningful. The movement can be described as one from a mechanistic to an organic structure.[10]

The mechanistic structure, typical of the large bureaucratic company, was compatible with a situation of stable markets and stable technology. It was characterized by highly specialized and separate jobs, coordination by a hierarchic supervisory authority, knowledge concentrated at the top of the hierarchy, primarily vertical integration, and work behavior governed by supervisors' communications. Such a system worked from the advent of mass production until recently. Its breakdown is related to changes in the world economy. Markets are no longer stable; with the advent of programmable automation, neither is technology.

The organic structure, with its inherent flexibility, is more adaptable to a situation of rapidly changing markets and technology. It is characterized by greater decentralization, coordination by mutual adjustment, knowledge located anywhere regardless of authority, lateral flow of information, and communication in the form of information and advice. A constantly changing environment demands a large range of responses from the organization. In such situations, it is beneficial for each element to possess more than one function, since each function may be performed in different ways with different combinations of elements. This need is being reflected in the expanding scope of jobs and the greater autonomy afforded those performing the jobs. Information systems should be designed to supply information to the point at which it is acted on. This need is reflected in the relocating of decision making further down the hierarchical structure. The inherent quality of the organic structure is its ability to deal better with uncertainty, which is precisely what characterizes the manufacturing environment today.

Handle the Union Response

For unionized facilities, the new technology has significant labor relations implications. IRC's research reveals an almost total absence of union resistance to technological change. Effective communications programs have convinced unions that computer-based technology is necessary to make firms competitive and thus enable them to provide jobs for the bulk of the work force. In the one case found of a strike, the dispute was not over the introduction of numerically controlled machining centers but over their manning, an example of the failure of management to plan adequately and communicate with the union.

In order to minimize labor-management conflict, it is essential to identify the possible areas of conflict: seniority, job classifications, bargaining unit work, compensation, economic security, and employee involvement. Next it is necessary to formulate a strategy for securing the changes management needs, as well as the means of resolving conflict: special joint labor-management committees or regular collective bargaining procedures.

Traditional seniority systems can be impediments to the efficient operation of programmable automation. Bumping provisions, which allow a senior worker to take the job of a junior one when the former loses his or her job, can undermine management's ability to place and keep the most qualified workers on the new technology and make it difficult to maintain a stable skills bank and a flexible work force. Companies, however, were able to gain some relief on this issue. Recognizing the need to keep trained operators on advanced processes, some unions have agreed to taking those jobs out of the bumping sequence. Seniority job-bidding systems also diminish management's ability to place the most qualified persons on jobs. Union relentlessness on this issue can be dealt with by requiring bidders for jobs to pass qualification tests.

The greatest advantage of programmable automation is the flexibility in manufacturing that it permits; that, in turn, requires greater flexibility within the work force. Where labor agreements have narrow job classifications, individuals are restricted in the tasks they may perform. Unions generally resist management's efforts to broaden jobs because they believe that this diminishes job security.

One way to expand classifications without incurring union opposition is to include setup work in the jobs. Since workers like the broadened jobs, unions are constrained from resisting the movement. An added advantage is changed worker attitudes. Since the worker has set the job up, he or she gets a feeling of ownership rather than the former attitude of "I only run the machine."

By changing the nature of work, computer-based technology is posing serious problems in determining whether a job belongs inside or outside the bargaining unit. Some workers are relying less on traditional skills and tools and more on computers to perform their jobs, and some argue that this change in the nature of the work should exclude it from the bargaining unit. Unions, fearing an erosion of their strength, claim that the work should remain a bargaining unit task.

A typical problem concerns who does the programming of the programmable machine tools. The usual solution is a compromise: off-line programming is done by salaried employees but that on-line by bargaining unit personnel. For example, at a steel company that was introducing a $200 million continuous casting process controlled by three levels of computers, the issue of what work belonged in the bargaining unit was resolved through compromise. Level one, computer control of individual machines, will be handled by electrical technicians, who are union members. Level two, computer control of the metallurgical process, will have some bargaining unit personnel, plus engineers. Level three, the overall process automation, will be run by nonbargaining unit personnel.

Some unions are responding to employers' demands for broadened jobs with counterdemands for job upgrades and higher pay rates. Where jobs have been expanded, they should be upgraded and their pay levels raised. But pay adjustments should be made only where they are objectively warranted, not as bribes for union acquiescence. Companies have resisted the temptation to bump rates up merely to overcome union resistance to job classification changes. Management moving to a team approach should consider a skills-based compensation structure.

The compensation problems associated with new technology are minimal except for those related to incentive systems. Programmable automation renders traditional individual incentive pay systems invalid because production is no longer controlled by the workers. Individual incentive systems, however, have become ingrained in the shop floor culture, and unions are loathe to agree to their abandonment. Companies consequently are searching for group incentive schemes with which to replace individual ones. In one case, a group incentive was based on avoidance of downtime.

Naturally unions are concerned about the job dislocation impact of technological change and often seek some form of income or job security as a condition for cooperating with management on its implementation. But one can guarantee only what can be guaranteed. The recently concluded Ford and General Motors agreements with the United Auto Workers guarantee jobs against loss due to technological change but not against market declines. As long as the companies can lay off workers when demand falls, they can afford the technological job security guarantee because they will use manpower planning—usually normal and speeded-up attrition—to prevent job loss due to automation.

Employee involvement activities facilitate the introduction and efficient operation of programmable automation because they create an atmosphere of trust and credibility between labor and management and provide a forum for educating labor about the company's economic condition. Attitudes toward involvement do vary greatly among companies and unions and even within a company or union. A history of hostile labor-management relations at a plant makes local leaders suspicious of company motives, and it takes time and special efforts by management to engender new attitudes.

One case was particularly remarkable because it represented the conversion of a hostile labor-management relationship, with a good deal of downtime due to work stoppages, to a cooperative one. Management concluded that its new integrated manufacturing system would not work unless the entire culture of the plant was changed. To that end, the union's involvement in the project for technological change was solicited. The local agreed; the union became part of the project and was kept fully informed at all stages. Union representatives—the chief steward and the stewards of each of the production departments—were on the planning committee. Regular meetings with employees were held to report on progress and difficulties encountered. Management's efforts paid off. A much more cooperative industrial relations climate emerged, evidenced by a dramatic 75 percent drop in time lost due to work stoppages.

Unions will cooperate in employee involvement efforts only if there is a role for them in the program. When they participate, the traditional adversarial labor-management relationship will give way to a more cooperative one.

Conclusions

The major lesson that emerges from the IRC study of company experience is that if the transition to computer-based manufacturing is to be accomplished smoothly, management must plan carefully, and the employee relations function should be involved in this planning from the beginning. The introduction of the new technology is almost always gradual, so there is time for an effective planning effort.

Introducing computer-based technology poses new challenges to the human resource function. Workers naturally are concerned with job security, and management must fashion programs to ameliorate adverse employment effects of new technology. Technological change also presents new opportunities for the employee relations function: to change the way work is organized, to achieve involvement of employees in pursuit of enterprise goals, and to reverse the traditional adversarial labor-management relationships. Companies that have reaped the greatest benefits from the new technology have adhered to the human resource imperatives in introducing it: plan, communicate, train, deal with displacement, change the structure of work, and intelligently handle the union response.

1
Computer-based Technologies

Various computer-based technologies are encountered in the manufacturing process. The two major families of programmable automation are computer-aided design (CAD) and computer-aided manufacturing (CAM). The latter encompasses industrial robots, computerized numerical control machines (CNC), automated materials-handling systems (AMHS), automated storage and retrieval systems (ASRS), and vision systems. Flexible manufacturing systems result from the combination of several types of computer-based equipment, most commonly a computerized NC machine, an industrial robot, and an automated materials-handling system, all operating under central computer control. The use of programmable automation for design, manufacturing, and management in an integrated system is often referred to as computer-integrated manufacturing (CIM).[1]

At each of the sixteen companies studied, one or more examples of programmable automation were in use. Many of the companies operated flexible manufacturing systems featuring computerized numerical control machines and industrial robots. CIM was rare, with one or perhaps two employers running such programs.

Computer-aided Design

CAD systems are computerized drafting tables. Instead of creating drawings on paper with pen, compass and ruler, the drafter or design engineer generates the desired lines and shapes on a video screen by typing at a computer keyboard.[2] CAD technology greatly increases user productivity because drawings can be replicated within a design, transferred from one part of a design to another, scaled up or down or rotated, and stored in computer memory for future reference.

These attributes are particularly important to designers and engineers at companies such as electronics manufacturers that produce products with complex design characteristics or companies such as aircraft or instrument manufacturers or defense contractors that must manufacture to exact specifications. In the latter case, companies often link CAD terminals to computerized machine tools to ensure a precise translation of design criteria into manufacturing specifications. A shipbuilding company established such a system to ensure that steel slabs were cut and pipes bent to the precise tolerances demanded by the nature of the product, as well as by the government.

In its more advanced form, CAD is the foundation of computer-aided engineering, allowing engineers to submit potential product designs to computer-simulated performance and stress tests. Automotive engineers in particular rely heavily on this tool so that they do not have to build prototypes of designs being considered for development.

Industrial Robots

The Robotics Institute of America, a trade association of robot manufacturers, consultants, and users, defines an industrial robot as a "reprogrammable, multifunctional manipulator designed to move materials, parts, tools, or specialized devices through variable programmed motions for the performance of a variety of tasks." Although robots have come to symbolize technological innovation in the workplace, they are among the simplest forms of computer-based manufacturing equipment. Industrial robots are the least costly form of programmable automation, and they can be used in many different ways. Even so, companies outside the automotive industry use relatively few robots. The automobile industry itself accounts for about 40 percent of the robots in manufacturing. A chemical company with about 100,000 workers had only thirty-five robots at the time of the study, and most others had fewer. An electronics instrument company of about the same size was using only seventeen robots. The best estimates of the number of industrial robots in the United States in 1986 put the total at a little over 20,000.

Industrial robots most commonly are used for materials handling, spray painting, welding, and machine loading. Robots also manipulate laboratory glassware and instruments as part of a chemical testing process, build printed circuit boards, and handle hazardous materials, specifically samples from a nuclear laboratory. Assembly work by robots is still at a relatively early stage because technology has yet to develop robot arms sufficiently flexible or sensitive to process parts of various sizes, dimensions, and weights. An aircraft manufacturer claimed that it could not use robots extensively because they cannot work to the close tolerances needed in aircraft production.

The current limitations of industrial robots have led to the redesign of some products to facilitate robotic assembly. Companies are designing parts to snap together in modules rather than screw together, a more difficult operation for robots. Where screws cannot be eliminated, their size or shape is being standardized so the robot can handle them more easily. Employers are finding that the emphasis on design for robotic assembly is helping to improve the efficiency of manual assembly operations as well.

Generally employers purchase stock robots and customize them to fit their specific needs. An aircraft manufacturer that was using a robot for laying up material for laminating composites bought a standard one and then developed the end effector itself. A few companies build their own robots. Several companies operated robotics laboratories in which robots were subjected to a variety of tests and potential applications were explored. At other companies, the robot was directly installed on the shop floor in a specific application, and modifications were made on the line. Companies that followed the latter course believe that the capital investment should begin supporting its purchase immediately. Managers must justify their robot purchases on conventional return-on-investment (ROI) criteria. Because ROI analysis fails to capture some of the technology's benefits, such as its flexibility and higher quality, and therefore tends to underestimate its true return, robots are being adopted only slowly in industry.

Traditional accounting systems are charged with being a major roadblock to more rapid movement by American industry to programmable automation. According to *Industry Week*, companies are being stymied by the "continued use of obsolete cost-justification tools in assessing investments in advanced technology."[3] By focusing on direct labor costs, companies fail to measure other benefits of new technology, such as improved product reliability, that stem from the accuracy of a programmed machine tool. Greater reliability may mean less inspection and less material waste.

Time also is a crucial factor. A General Electric facility reports that time savings proved to be the greatest benefit of CAD/CAM: "It used to take seven to eight weeks for our people to manufacture a prototype . . . but [now] . . . we can design the same prototype within a week's time."[4]

Numerically Controlled Machine Tools

The oldest form of programmable automation is the NC machine tool that can shape or cut metal according to programmed instructions. More than 100,000 such machine tools are in operation. The development of numerical control was fostered by the U.S. Air Force "to help produce complex parts for aircraft which were difficult to make reliably and economically with a manually guided machine tool."[5] Some students of technology charge that the NC machine tool was favored over other potential methods because it removed control of production from the skilled machinists.[6]

The microcomputer revolution of the past decade has brought the CNC machine tool, which is more reliable than its older NC counterparts. It also has somewhat reskilled the machinist. With the NC machine, the writing and editing of programs was performed by programmers off-line; with the CNC, some of that work can be done at the machine by the operator.

There are numerous applications of NC and CNC machine tools. In most cases, engineers and managers extol them not because of their productivity but because of their contributions to flexibility and product reliability. The greatest advantage of CNC at a bearing plant is the time saved in switching from machining one size of bearing to another—from an average of thirty hours on the old automatic screw machine to a half-hour of reprogramming. This time saving is extremely important since orders for a particular size of bearing are generally quite small. An aircraft manufacturing plant was developing a series of flexible machining cells that would use seventy-nine NCs controlled by a central computer. The machines are being manufactured specifically for the company by an American electrical-electronics products company. This company's primary objective in using the new technology is product quality, obviously vital in aircraft manufacturing.

A company that has suffered a decline in demand for its traditional product has been able to move into a related product line by installing computerized machining cells. Each CNC machining cell, purchased from a major U.S. machine tool manufacturer, has a 90-tool magazine capacity and can produce 165 discrete parts. They represent a form of flexible automation, with automatic work changing, tool changing, part indexing, chip removal, and fault detector capabilities.

Automated Materials-handling Systems

The physical link between workstations in a computer-based manufacturing environment is the AMHS. It transports materials to and from workstations and elsewhere within a factory by automated guided vehicle, powered conveyor, or rail cart operating under central computer control. The computer orchestrates and tracks the movement of materials throughout the production system in a way that minimizes both machine and worker idleness. The AMHS not only serves as the backbone of flexible, or computer-based, manufacturing but also generates data that can be used to improve the company's materials management process.

Most companies studied have some type of AMHS, although its scope and complexity varied. At an aircraft plant, a small, circular overhead rail system carries sheets of graphite laminate to a robotic cutter. In contrast, at a consumer electronics manufacturing facility, a long and complex network of powered conveyors and rail systems moves work in process from one assembly station to the next, delivering materials according to the assemblers' needs as determined by a computer and in a sequence that eliminates bottlenecks in the production process. This AMHS was designed to accommodate a variety of product designs with only minor adjustments. This system, as well as some found elsewhere, automatically routes to repair stations products the computer identifies as defective.

Automated Storage and Retrieval Systems

An ASRS is a computer-based warehouse, which often stands at the front end of an AMHS. A computer codes each item as it enters the storage facility, mechanically places the item within the structure using a network of elevators and transport vehicles, and records the item's precise location in its memory. The system instantly provides management with up-to-the-minute data on inventory levels and characteristics and expedites handling of incoming and outgoing inventory. ASRSs were operating at several plants, and they were in the planning phase at others.

At an electronics plant, the ASRS consists of a six-story complex housing a network of computer-driven elevators and rail systems. A computer linked to the production process informs a worker that parts or materials are needed, and he or she then inputs these requirements into the ASRS. The ASRS delivers the goods to the factory floor where they are received by an automated guided vehicle, which transports them to the production line.

At a synthetic textile manufacturing plant, the ASRS takes a different shape. There the system consists of a network of overhead rails and elevators that move massive chemical tanks from a holding area into position to have their contents inserted into the production stream. When the contents of a tank are emptied, the tank is automatically returned to the holding area.

At an electrical components factory, the decision to install an ASRS was based on a need to remedy a specific problem rather than to increase the overall efficiency of the manufacturing process. The problem was that parts manufactured at workstations were getting lost or misplaced in storage before they reached the final assembly area. With the introduction of an ASRS, a computer routes the parts to a central storage facility after they are built and then automatically directs them to final assembly stations in the appropriate numbers and mixes. The cost of materials was substantially reduced and manufacturing productivity greatly increased.

Vision Systems

Vision systems rely on a combination of optical instruments and computers to perform a variety of tasks, including quality control and machine guidance. In quality-control applications, a computer checks the image of a part passing beneath a camera at an inspection point and compares it with the features of a properly manufactured part, which are stored in the computer's memory. If the actual and specified characteristics differ, the system rejects the part and routes it for repair. In a machine guidance application, of which there are several types, the system's optical capabilities are used to direct the movement of machine tools and robots or control the position of parts along a production line. Vision systems are among the most complex computer-based technologies, and we found only a few examples. They were most commonly used for quality-control purposes. Several companies believe that vision systems can contribute enormously to lowering production costs and raising quality, and these companies are developing simple systems as a launching point.

Computer-controlled Systems

Various other forms of programmable automation also were encountered. To a large extent, they fall into the category of computerized control systems. We visited plants that had installed automated continuous-casting processes. A steel company, for example, introduced a state-of-the-art continuous-casting process run with a multilevel computer system. (With the old method of production, molten steel had to be made into ingots, which were then processed through a slabbing mill. Continuous casting eliminates this stage of production by turning the liquid steel directly into semifinished slabs, billets, or blooms.) A synthetics plant was, in essence, a network of computer-operated and computer-controlled systems.

Most of the programmable automation we observed, whether CAD systems, robots, or CNC machines, was not integrated into an overall system; rather it can best be described as islands of automation. Some companies, however, are attempting to integrate these islands into flexible manufacturing systems and eventually to achieve CIM. This goal is being stymied by the lack of a common data base—the inability of the various pieces of programmable automation to communicate with each other—but this problem will be solved in time.

Implementation of Programmable Automation

Although companies take different routes when introducing programmable automation, the pattern of implementation is fairly uniform. A company starts with an island of automation—a single robot or computerized NC machine, for example—and then purchases additional pieces of computer-based automation that complement its existing stock. This incremental automation strategy is based on cost considerations, an organization's limited ability to absorb technological change in large doses in a short period of time, and the practical matter of integrating new technologies into an existing manufacturing process.

Many managers characterized the decision to install complex computer-based manufacturing technologies as difficult and risky, especially when the operation was running smoothly and profitably. The equipment is expensive and the cost of downtime high. Managers at several companies hedged their bets on programmable automation by maintaining some elements of manual operations so that if a highly integrated computer-based system breaks down, production can continue on a limited basis if there are enough hands around to do the job.

Some managers are reluctant to invest in new technology because it becomes outdated in a relatively short time—sometimes less than two years in the case of some industrial robots. Other companies are investing great amounts of money to automate as many of their operations as they can. One company admitted that perhaps it had overautomated some operations and neglected productivity gains that could have been achieved through work redesign and worker motivation. It fears that managers are substituting programmable automation for good human resource management practices. Its current philosophy is that a job should be automated only when the result will be a performance level that exceeds that of a highly motivated worker in a properly structured work setting.

The introduction of computerized manufacturing systems often is related to other changes in plant operations, such as just-in-time inventories. All the companies studied have moved to leaner in-process, as well as raw materials and parts, inventories. When interest rates were 3 percent, the size of inventories mattered much less; at today's interest rates, the cost of carrying excessive inventory becomes prohibitive. Computerized materials-handling and storage and retrieval systems aid management in holding inventories to a minimum.

Although the introduction of computer-based technology itself results in better quality, companies have gone well beyond this in their drive for improved product quality. For example, the adoption of programmable automation at an electrical products plant created a need for tighter tolerances in all parts. Not only did the company tighten up tolerances within its own plant, but it also worked with its suppliers in getting them to do the same on the parts they furnished. Company engineers went to the supplier plants to work with their engineers on the tightened standards. Ninety percent of the contractors responded positively and met the new standards, particularly since it allowed them to produce better products, which aided their sales to other companies. The minority that could not match the new standards were dropped as suppliers.

Companies are spending considerable sums of money on the research and development of programmable automation applications and therefore are interested in spreading the knowledge they have learned throughout their organizations. This process of technological diffusion is undertaken in a variety of ways. A computer/electronics company uses a combination of technology boards and rotating assignments, and a chemical company has a corporate robotics committee staffed by manufacturing, engineering, and employee relations personnel. Other companies have internal technology newsletters or periodic seminars where issues related to computer-based manufacturing are discussed.

Although the implementation of computer-based technology is a gradual process, it will continue because of the benefits that flow from it, all of them vital to companies' ability to compete in a global economy. An obvious benefit is increased productivity and thus reduced production costs. Another is improved product reliability. Time also is a crucial factor since a programmable machine tool can be reprogrammed in a fraction of the time required for retooling traditional technology. Thus perhaps the greatest long-run benefit of computer-based technology is that it provides the flexibility needed to respond quickly to market shifts. In effect, computer-based technology will enable batch production (low-volume production, which is characteristic of most U.S. manufacturing today), to achieve some of the advantages common to continuous process and mass production systems. Given the decline in product life cycles, it will enable all manufacturing to move from one product to another quickly, beneficial for company profits and for stability of employment as well.

2
Planning the Introduction of New Technology

Role of Employee Relations

The complexity and scope of the changes brought about by the new technology, along with its capital requirements, necessitate extensive planning to determine what, when, and where programmable automation will be introduced into the manufacturing process, as well as how the new technology will be implemented. Because technological innovation often forces changes in other modes of operation, such as the introduction of just-in-time inventory systems, its impact on organizational design also must be foreseen. Appropriate planning should ease the transition from old to new systems.

Ideally human resource planning should be an integral part of a company's program for the introduction of technological change. How the technology will alter the composition of the work force, for example, will affect recruitment, training, and transfer needs. According to a recent study, senior human resources executives believe that the employee relations function will become more heavily involved with operations, decisions, and company strategies.[1] "Nearly 80 percent of strategically oriented managers plan to devote major attention to the human resources link with business planning." Yet we found many instances in which the employee relations function was not brought into formulating policies and plans for the introduction of new technology. Employee relations, as a staff function, tended to enter the picture only when problems arose. In the high-tech areas of one company, manufacturing specifies when and what training is needed, and then employee relations designs the training program. In another company, the employee relations people are involved only to the extent of working with line management to reassign affected employees.

A survey of major companies conducted by one of the companies in our study revealed that none of them had developed and/or communicated a coherent policy statement regarding the employee relations issues associated with programmable automation. For companies in the study, the situation was similar. Although most companies have employee relations and communications policies, none seems to address the automation issue specifically. The company that conducted the survey decided that it needed to clarify and communicate its position on this issue.

This company is composed of autonomous divisions, so the corporate entity recommends positions to the divisions, which are given latitude to develop their own statements. The positions they develop, however, must support the company's established principles and be consistent with policies generated to address area-related employee relations matters. For example, the company adheres to the principle of providing employees with as much notice of new technology as possible and imparting full information to them. It recommends to its divisions that the following elements should be addressed in each business unit's position statement:

> That the use of automation is critical to its long-term competitive position and growth.

> That although some displacement may occur as a result of the introduction of new technology, management will make every effort to minimize its effects through the use of advance notice, attrition, and retraining.

> That management will address all issues concerning safety, compensation, and changes in job content relative to the introduction of new technology.

> That management will keep employees fully informed and involved in the process of introducing new technology and that, where applicable, it will seek the cooperation, involvement, and input of the unions representing the employees.

The realization that his company had no appropriate policy led one chief executive officer to form a task force to review the human resources implications of automation. As a result of that task force's study, the corporate employee relations department developed guidelines on the employee relations considerations in both factory and office automation. The guidelines, which apply to all domestic operations, enable line and staff people involved in planning and implementing factory and office automation to identify employee relations issues, such as displacement, training and retraining, job content analysis, compensation, changes in staffing, organization and the process of introducing new technology, psychological impacts, and health and safety considerations. The guidelines suggest that strategic, operational, and human resource planning must be part of a single integrated planning process.

The human resource function of a telecommunications manufacturer with an advanced technological planning process remained until recently largely reactive, with planning done by the line. At one of its plants, however, human resources is being upgraded and has become part of the strategic planning team. The ratio of human resources staff to employees has doubled, rising in one year from 1:150 to 1:72. Human resources is decentralized, and members of the department are integrated with the line in the various departments; in effect, the plant has a matrix organization. A major improvement is that the director of human resources now reports directly to the head of the business unit rather than to the controller.

Other companies too are upgrading the role of the employee relations function as they begin to realize the value of a coordinated planning process. An aircraft manufacturer is doing a great deal of long-range planning for the development of a highly technologically sophisticated manufacturing process. Human resources planning is part of the overall planning process. In the first phase of the program, a human resource plan was developed and integrated with the strategic plan. During phase 2, the human resources function will be involved in the training of people to operate and maintain the new technology.

Similar measures to involve the employee relations function in planning are being taken at the plants of other companies. The function thus becomes responsible for aiding in the selection and training of employees for new operations and for minimizing the human costs associated with bringing new technology on-line by using attrition to trim the work force, filling in with temporary workers during the interim period, and transferring surplus employees to other departments.

For other companies, particularly those with considerable experience in introducing new technology, human resources planning for technological change is nothing new. They have adopted as a principle the minimization of employee displacement. Obviously long-range human resources planning is of paramount importance to companies pursuing full-employment policies.

A chemical company has had a continual program of productivity improvement, which always has reduced the labor content of products. The company has not pursued this effort surreptitiously but has been open with employees. It plans for career movement by hiring people with a variety of abilities who can perform different jobs and by deliberately reducing the number of job categories so that people can move more easily to other jobs. The company, thus, has the flexibility it needs to undertake new ventures and the ability to move people as processes change. In order to avoid displacement, the company may choose from a variety of options: intraplant transfers, extending the right to employees to transfer to other plants in the area, carrying excess employees for a period, and cutting down on subcontracting.

For many years, a computer manufacturer has incorporated human resources planning in its divisions' strategic and operational planning. Responsibility for human resource planning rests within the corporate personnel function, but much of the actual planning occurs at the divisional level. Within its divisions, special human resource planning coordinators participate in plan preparation, especially when issues of implementation are being considered. Corporate planning specialists work with their counterparts at the division level to be certain that all implications are thought through and that steps are taken to ameliorate any long-term adverse effects. In a two-year plan developed by personnel and operations management, resource flows were examined, and human resources were evaluated from the point of view of skills. Through this system, manufacturing and personnel cooperate in determining how change will be introduced in terms of its effect on employees.

The general management philosophy of a company manufacturing instruments has had a crucial influence on its introduction of new technology. The philosophy provides that employees are not to be affected adversely by innovation. Generally anyone made redundant has been found another job at a comparable level. Occasionally this has required more than routine efforts—for example, getting all the managers within a division to work together to find suitable openings for displaced employees. Only if the division cannot solve the problem does the corporate employee relations staff become involved. On occasion, given its philosophy, the company delayed introducing new technology until the human resource problems were worked out. (Given the more competitive environment now confronting the company, one wonders whether it will be able to maintain such a policy in the future.)

One company indicated that its timetable for effecting major technological change always allows for long-range planning and dealing with displacement problems. Another company noted that the human aspect of new technology has not been a problem, largely because of the growth environment in which the new technology was introduced. A third reported that it is not engaged in long-range human resource planning because it does not believe that a CIM revolution is on the horizon. This company, however, although it has introduced pieces of computerized technology, may be jeopardizing its future by not seeing their eventual evolution into a system as others push ahead of it to greater efficiency and flexibility.

In unionized settings, the role of the employee relations function takes on an added dimension: it must communicate with the union and attempt to enlist its support for innovation. In an appliance plant, employee relations was involved in planning from the beginning, keeping both the union and the employees informed of all developments. Human resources matters were a major focus of the project, and employee relations provided an open, honest, and consistent communications plan. These human resources matters were measured throughout the project, and employee relations created enriched jobs and, in some plant operations, autonomous teams.

Companies that have both unionized and unorganized plants indicate that one policy adhered to in conjunction with the introduction of new technology is the containment of unionism—that is, remaining nonunion where unions do not already exist. In facilities in which employees are represented, management aims to deal fairly and constructively with the unions. Management generally, however, is determined not to allow labor relations problems to interfere with the introduction of new technology. The formation of specific industrial relations policies is usually left to plant-level management.

It seems that the more planning that is required and the more change that is anticipated with new technology, the more likely it is that the employee relations function will take on a proactive role. As greater strides are taken in revolutionizing work processes for more efficient manufacturing technologies, we should begin to see this enlargement in the role of the employee relations function becoming more widespread. One of the plants we visited has gone so far as to treat it as a line function, integrating employee relations people into manufacturing operations.

Employee Involvement

In IRC's survey of opinion on the introduction of programmable automation, respondents from both the United States and Britain ranked the importance of employee understanding and acceptance higher than employee involvement in planning. Respondents indicated that although employees need not be directly involved in planning, it is imperative that employers take employees into their confidence at every stage of the introduction process. Nevertheless, both union and industry respondents in the United States note the importance of involving employees in all stages of the process, from planning through implementation. An industry respondent said:

> If American workers are included in plans and implementations of robotics, they will sponsor the effort and the results will be more valuable, more productive, because of their input.

A respondent who represents a trade union viewpoint said:

> The Japanese include their workers in the implementation and use of systems. They have found that the full potential of the new systems is more quickly realized when the workers are involved from the beginning. U.S. companies could greatly speed the rate at which full efficiency is achieved if the workers are involved.

The case studies too indicated that positive attitudes toward new technology were correlated with employee involvement in its planning and implementation. Workers who participated in the debugging process came to appreciate the capabilities of the technology and their role in operating it.

Where new technology was simply imposed on workers, they resented it, feared it, and tended to resist it. At a plant using nuclear materials, robotization was undertaken to reduce worker exposure to radiation in pulling the waste out of the system. Even so, acceptance of the automated system became a problem largely because the employees did not view it as being "their" system; they had not been consulted about it.

In most companies, employee involvement is limited to implementation and does not include design and planning for new technology. In some, even that participation comes only through the suggestion system rather than any formal employee involvement mechanism. One company, however, reported good results using a suggestion system because management takes it seriously. Employees even suggested how robots might better do their jobs.

A more typical situation is represented by the application of robots in the chemical company with an interdivisional robotics group. Line management of any unit initiates the movement to robotics by going to the robotics group for assistance in getting the project off the ground. Line management is responsible for informing employees about the new technology. The employee relations function is not involved in implementation, which becomes the responsibility of a specially established implementation committee. First, a laboratory mock-up of the process is set up by the robotics group. Then plant engineers are brought in for their input, as are selected operators. The latter are chosen carefully and are expected to be knowledgeable in their jobs, respected by fellow workers, and willing to participate in the group's activities. Equipment vendors train the technical personnel, who in turn train supervisors and the selected operators. These operators then train the other operators. An important lesson learned by this company is the need for continuity of personnel during the implementation process because replacements who join a project in midcourse often lack the enthusiasm of the original participants.

Employee involvement in technological planning is most evident in facilities using a sociotechnical approach to the organization of work, with the autonomous work teams becoming part of the planning process. At one such plant manufacturing specialized cable, the employees are consulted early in the preimplementation process; thus they have a sense of ownership of the process. The team concept complements the changing design of the product, and the teams shape new technology by identifying problems to be overcome. This also is part of the management philosophy: that the primary resource for production is people. There is a storehouse of knowledge in the work force, and traditional management used very little of it. At this plant, design engineering listens to the production employees, and the teams help establish standards.

The special nature of the sociotechnical organization means that the human resources function also is involved in planning, including process design. In fact, human resources is not treated as simply a staff function but as part of line management. The teams work on long-range planning, helping to decide such questions as whether updated equipment is needed and how many people are required for operations. The teams can perform such functions because they have the information needed for decision making, such as precisely how much it costs to manufacture the product and the price at which it is selling. The teams also help implement new processes.

In some organized situations, management has worked closely with the unions, to the point of including shop stewards on the committees planning and/or implementing the introduction of the new processes. In one case at the conclusion of the project, management asked the union to evaluate the planning process from its point of view. On the positive side, that evaluation stressed that everybody was committed to quality, that the hourly employees and the company worked together, that when problems arose management listened more freely than it had in the past, that informative meetings had been held, and that work areas were improved. But the union said that management should have solicited the hourly employees' ideas about how to design the equipment and processes. When questioned, management indicated that it agreed with the union: the workers have learned over the years that designs emanating from engineering must be creatively adapted on the plant floor if they are to be utilized effectively; had workers been involved, their ideas could have helped the design engineers avoid problems that did arise later in the operational stage.

Another company that manufactures sophisticated office equipment had explicitly recognized this experience resource in advance and had had hourly employees working with design engineers on a project. Although the engineers at first resented the intrusion of the workers onto what they regarded as their turf, most of their opposition dissipated as they came to recognize that the workers could make helpful suggestions.

Employee involvement at this company takes place through the team approach. The teams engage in planning and examine future issues in human resource management, including those related to technology. Manpower planning also falls into the teams' purview. The planning process starts when the operating people identify a technological change, such as the installation of a robot. They inform the manager of the industrial relations function, who contacts the union leadership, and a meeting is held. Management puts forth the reasons for the new technology, its timing and its impact, and the union leaders are shown the equipment. (At the request of the union leadership, introduction of new technology has been delayed on occasion so as not to occur during union election campaigns.) Next management meets with the steward and workers of the affected area. The work force helps plan for the new technology through a team composed of people from the affected unit, supplemented by employees from other parts of the organization as needed.

In the appliance plant that followed a program of including employees in the planning process for implementing an entirely new automated process, both the union and employee response to the new technology was decidedly favorable. Data supplied on the plant's annual attitude surveys disclosed much more positive feelings about job security, job satisfaction, participation, the plant climate, and the effectiveness of communications following the change (table 2–1).

Employee involvement in technological planning must have visible results in management's acceptance and incorporation of practical ideas. An electronics instruments plant that sought to secure worker input into its system design found itself unable to use the ideas contributed. Management had little room to redesign the operation along the lines suggested because it had bought a software package but had no expertise for modifying it. Employees became disillusioned and reacted negatively to the new system. Management learned a lesson from this experience and hired an expert on software modification so that, in the future, employee suggestions could be incorporated into new systems.

Conclusion

Planning is essential for a smooth transition to computer-based technology. Those organizations that have included human resources planning as an integral part of overall strategic planning have been the most successful. Given the extended gestation period for introducing new technology, moreover, effective long-range planning is quite feasible.

Table 2–1
Employee Attitudes, before and after Introduction of New Technology

	Positive		Negative	
	1981	1984	1981	1984
Job security	22.8%	66.2%	42.2%	6.1%
Participation	26.0	42.4	32.8	15.7
Climate	23.0	45.0	30.0	11.2
Job satisfaction	22.5	52.6	40.8	11.5
Quality of communication	45.0	54.5	11.0	1.8
Effectiveness of communication	34.0	51.6	16.0	5.7

3
Communications

Company Communication Efforts

Communications and advance notice are vital to the planning process for technological change. The introduction of new technology, or any other innovation in the workplace, induces anxiety among employees. Concerns about job security, ability to handle new or altered jobs, and work group integrity normally arise, and they tend to provoke resistance to change. An employer seeking to secure the cooperation of its work force, and where organized, its union, in introducing computer-based automation must first assuage fears about the impact of the technology on jobs and work life.

The companies studied communicated well with employees on the need for introducing new technology. Through their openness, they secured employee acceptance of change and willingness to work with the new processes. The almost total absence of employee and union resistance to computer-based technology is testimony to management's communications efforts. There was only one strike related to new technology, and this was due, in part, to inadequate communications.

The communications programs varied among the companies. Not surprisingly, there were instances of a divergence of views within management as to the type of communications strategy to pursue. At a telecommunications manufacturer, line management wanted to consider the installation of computer-based technology an event, requiring special meetings with union officials in preparation for negotiations to reach new understandings. The industrial relations staff opposed this strategy, arguing that by characterizing programmable automation as unique rather than a new phase in a long history of technological change, the company would build a union case for management concessions in exchange for its accommodation to the new technology. An internal management debate led to a compromise position—not making something special of the new technology but meeting with the union leaders to explain it. That meeting was productive, and the programmable automation was well received.

The precise strategy of communications varied among the companies. An office equipment manufacturer has found that a structured communications program best serves its interests. First, senior management informs the industrial relations department that the new manufacturing technologies will be installed. The department then notifies the union leadership of the

18 • *Computerized Manufacturing and Human Resources*

decisions, and the parties meet to discuss the timetable of the action and the workplace implications. The next step in the process is to hold a meeting between plant management and shop floor union representatives, mainly the stewards. These sessions are designed to gain leadership understanding and, hence, support of the new technology. Finally, plant management presents the plan for the new technology to the work force.

At a plant converting its warehouse to ASRS, there was no direct employee involvement in formulating policies and plans for the introduction of the technology, but everyone was kept fully apprised of it. Management policy dictates that employees be given at least six weeks' notice of impending change, but in this case, notice was given much earlier. Employees were informed of this change and other aspects of plant operations through an existing communications program. This program consists of two large meetings each year at which the president speaks on the state of the company. The general managers of various operations also hold meetings. In addition, some 500 small group meetings of twenty-five to thirty people are held for hourly and salaried employees. Through these sessions, employees are kept up to date on company developments, including technological change.

One company followed the three-pronged pattern of communications—managers, employees, and union. Once the managers were informed about impending change, they explained what was coming to their subordinates. For the union, there was a slide presentation to the leadership, explaining the need for change, its nature and characteristics, and its impact on the work force. In one case with a major innovation, management explained that imports were threatening the company's old products, and for it to survive, production time had to be cut and new products and processes introduced. At that time, the combination of recession in the economy and the flood of imports had resulted in 900 workers being on layoff. Management's claims to the union—that the new technology and improved products, while substantially reducing the labor required per unit, would lead to higher total employment—were subsequently proved in practice.

Forms of Communication

Usually all types of communication are used: written, as well as meetings with formal presentations, including slide presentations and mockups of the new equipment. With the spread of employee involvement programs, however, work group meetings increasingly have become a major communication channel. Since the work groups meet regularly, information on the progress of the technology implementation and problems being encountered, to which work groups may have some solutions, can be presented continuously.

This type of personal, face-to-face communication was the procedure followed at a telecommunications products plant that was not organized. On each shift, one-hour sessions were held at which managers and engineers reviewed the entire economic and technical situation in which the plant found itself. They talked to the hourly employees as if they were professionals, explaining market share, identifying the competitors, and pointing to the need for CIM. They stressed that the company required its employees' help in effectuating change and admitted that mistakes would be made in the process of automating production. From management's point of view, the greatest need was to establish credibility with employees. All efforts were directed toward that end. Subsequent events showed that the communications program was a success; when serious technical problems with the new technology emerged, the work force cooperated fully in the difficult debugging process.

With a good communications effort and a program to aid those whose jobs were eliminated, one company was able to gain employee acceptance of a shutdown of an operation for economic reasons. Management wanted to eliminate the machine shop within a plant because it was cheaper to buy than make components. The message conveyed to the employees was that the machine shop was pulling down the whole plant. The fact that the machine shop included the highest-level production jobs held by the most senior workers could have been a major stumbling block, but management overcame it with generous early retirement and the fact that those transferred to other jobs were given rate protection for an extended period of time. As a result of management's explanations of the need to close the operation and its assistance to the affected workers, neither the employees nor their union raised objections to closing the machine shop.

Creating a New Industrial Relations Climate

Probably one of the most difficult tasks for management is to introduce advanced technology into a workplace in which labor and management historically have been at odds. The communications effort must not only overcome employees' anxieties concerning new technology but also must change the labor-management climate, particularly employee antagonism toward management.

The appliance division of a major consumer goods manufacturer had to meet such a challenge when it launched a $40 million program dedicated to making it the industry's lowest-cost, highest-quality producer of a particular item. Its efforts rested on three pillars: product (to redesign the appliance to ensure quality and attractiveness to consumers), process (to introduce a computer-based manufacturing system), and people (to achieve a less adversarial labor-management relationship).

Management realized at the outset that worker cooperation was critical to the program's success, especially the desired improvement in product quality. It also understood that in the light of the parties' historic stormy relationship, manifested by frequent unauthorized work stoppages, such cooperation would not easily be achieved. Management decided that the key to reversing the negative attitudes of union officials and members had to be communications. Its first step in this direction was to meet with local union leadership in order to describe the entire program of product and process change and to outline its anticipated job effects.

Management continued to communicate with union leaders as the program progressed and placed union representatives, that is, shop stewards, on the committees responsible for managing the transition to computer-based manufacturing. Additionally meetings between supervisors and the hourly work force were held regularly, and the production workers knew the status of the change. The company's discussions with union officials and workers purposely avoided direct or even veiled threats of additional layoffs or a plant closing if cooperation were not forthcoming. Management was committed to securing cooperation on a voluntary basis in order to effect a lasting change in the labor relations climate.

The meetings evolved into such a positive process that union officials claimed credit for them during the local's election campaign. Management did not challenge them on this point; it was more concerned with maintaining the new more cooperative labor-management relationship than winning kudos for having initiated it.

The company used employee attitude surveys to monitor the impact of its communications strategy and found higher levels of employee satisfaction in the areas of job security, participation, climate, jobs, and communication. With the production technology and a revitalized economy, the company gathered an increased market share for its product. Higher sales mitigated the displacement effect of the technology, and all who had been laid off during the previous two years of recession were recalled. While the company highlighted the greater job security flowing from the product and process change, it also warned the union that advanced technologies in other product lines and plants might result in job losses in the future.

The communications effort at this plant was successful. Production and sales were up, everyone was recalled to work, and employees' attitudes toward their jobs had improved considerably. Indicative of the new industrial relations climate was the fact that bargaining unit workers on the plant floor were wearing company T-shirts, rather rare in unionized situations. The new attitudes were also reflected in a new labor-management relationship, which had moved from fiercely adversarial to much more cooperative. Testifying to this was the fact that there was a 75 percent reduction in hours lost due to work stoppages.

Failure to Communicate Adequately

A virtually antithetical case emerged at another plant with a long history of adversarial labor-management relations. This case provides evidence that the failure to communicate adequately with the work force when introducing programmable automation can raise resistance levels. The company, a transportation equipment components manufacturer, decided to invest in computerized NC equipment in order to expand its product line, necessary because demand for its main product had fallen sharply. The market decline was so precipitous that the plant's hourly work force had fallen from 2,000 to 1,000, and there was a good chance that the facility would close if the company did not develop an alternative product.

The computerized equipment represented a leap in manufacturing technology for the plant, and the organized work force was apprehensive about its introduction. Although the company informed the workers that the CNC machines were critical to its drive to produce a different product competitively, it had no formal communications program and did not share economic and financial data supporting its case. The union leadership was said to understand the need for new technology but for political reasons felt constrained from endorsing it.

The company insisted that the union agree to work rules changes that would allow machine tool operators to perform more than one task. Under existing work rules, an operator performed one task and was responsible for a single machine. This rule had made sense under the old single-purpose machines, but the new CNCs could perform forty-six operations. Management's demand for relaxed work rules, in concert with a request for other contract concessions, but without sufficient explanations to the employees, precipitated a strike that lasted three and one-half weeks before the union acceded to a broadened job for CNC operators. (This was the only strike resulting from the introduction of technology at any company studied.)

This strike was attributable to many causes, but the absence of a concerted communication program to establish a climate conducive to the acceptance of change was a major contributing factor. The work force did not understand the overriding need for the new technology, the nature of the technology, or the more flexible work force utilization dictated by it. Nor did the company make any special effort to alter its employees' historic distrust of management's motives and actions.

Collective Bargaining Requirements

In some unionized situations, the employer's responsibility to communicate with employees and the union prior to introducing a technological change is specified in the labor-management agreement.

At a telecommunications manufacturer, the contract requires notification when technological change will result in displacing ten or more employees or changing the jobs of ten or more employees by establishing a different labor grade. The company must notify the union as soon as planning is sufficiently advanced for definitive proposals to be tabled and must update the information provided as new developments arise and new modifications are made. Meetings are to be arranged to discuss the situation and to provide pertinent data about the nature of the change; the approximate date on which the company proposes to effect the change; the approximate number, type, and location of employees likely to be affected by the change; and the effects the change may be expected to have on the employees. A more complex program of communications and consultation is set out in an automotive collective bargaining agreement.

Technological innovation has been a continuous process in this industry, and labor and management consequently have considerable experience dealing with technological change. Twenty years ago, the parties developed a policy issued as a "Statement on Technological Change." It defines the process by which management informs the union and issues are resolved. Administering the process is the National Committee on Technological Progress, a body composed of three management and three union representatives. It meets monthly to discuss technological developments within the company and their impact on the scope of bargaining units. The committee also discusses matters concerning advancing technology that may be referred to it by local managements or unions.

The statement sets forth means of resolving disputes arising from new technology. Where the initial introduction of a new or advanced technology at a plant location may cause a shift of work from represented to nonrepresented employees, affect the job responsibilities of represented employees, or otherwise affect the scope of the bargaining unit, plant management must discuss the matter with the shop committee. Plant management describes to the shop committee the extent to which the technological changes may affect the work performed by union members. The chairman of the committee and the international union are provided a written description of the technology, the equipment being introduced, their intended uses, and the anticipated installation dates. The statement specifies that "comments by the Shop Committee concerning the information provided will be carefully evaluated by the Local Management in accordance with the Corporation's policy relative to the assignment of work which comes within the scope and context of that normally assigned to represented employees at the plant location."

Settlements made by the local parties concerning the assignment of work functions between represented and nonrepresented employees in relation to the new or advanced technology are forwarded to the international union and corporate headquarters. Such agreements are then reviewed by the National Committee on Technological Progress within thirty days. If either party does not approve the settlement following its review by the national committee, the subject matter in dispute is referred to the management/shop committee step of the grievance procedure and then processed in accordance with the applicable provisions of the grievance procedure.

4
Reactions to New Technology

Despite the importance of new technology to American industry's regaining its competitive position, some companies have been slow to introduce computer-based technology, in part because they fear employee resistance. Such fears are highly exaggerated. To the contrary, the employee response often is positive. Usually, however, employees, particularly at the production level, display a neutral reaction to new technology, neither embracing it nor rejecting or being overwhelmed by it.

Employer behavior is a significant influence on worker reaction to new technology. When a company projects an image of concern with employee welfare, the response is more likely to be positive. The degree to which employees are not fearful of losing their jobs is the key factor in their attitudes toward change. As to be expected, the greater is the job security, the lower is the level of worker anxiety.[1] Job security is greatest in plants in which employment is increasing or at least stable. Although workers realize that they may be displaced from their present jobs and have to do others, as long as they believe that they will have comparably paying ones, they tend to accept change and even contribute ideas for still greater efficiency.

Even within a given company, attitudes toward new technology can vary from one plant to another. One company found that resistance tends to be greatest where there is a lack of adequate maintenance and electronic skills needed to support computer-based technology. This problem tends to be found in older plants and has been solved in some of them by contracting out maintenance functions. In fact, a major criterion guiding this company's priorities in the application of new technology is the receptivity of the plant work force.

Employee reactions are also influenced by the nature of the particular technology. Machinists resent the deskilling involved in the switchover to NC machines, particularly when their work is restricted and they do no programming. On the other hand, where change relieves them of heavy physical labor, the employees look forward to it. Robots often were first placed in hostile environments, and so were usually welcomed by employees. In one plant, a hot and dirty job—loading a die caster—was robotized because the workers so disliked it that anyone on it would seek a transfer as soon as he had accumulated enough seniority to bump someone else.

Change also is welcomed where it makes jobs more interesting—for instance, when preventive maintenance is added to jobs or when workers rotate among jobs. Some workers, however, experience difficulty in adjusting to a situation in which they cannot identify "their" work.

The pace of change is another important determinant of reaction to it. In most cases, technological change has been gradual, and only a portion of the work force has been affected at any one time. As some workers saw others adjust to change, they accepted new technology easily when it was introduced into their own operations.

Positive employee response to new technology, however, has not been universal. Some plants reported difficulty, despite active communication efforts, in convincing older employees that change will work to their benefit. Benefits tend to be long run, but older workers naturally have a short-run outlook. Even extensive training in working with new processes was not always successful, for some old-timers simply preferred the old way.

The importance of employees' perceiving that management is concerned with their well-being is well illustrated in a case in which those perceptions were decidedly negative. Over the years, a hard-nosed plant management had engaged in the types of behavior, such as scheduling layoffs just before Christmas, that undermine employee faith in management. This attitude, in turn, induced resistance to change when it came. No amount of explanation of the need for new technology or assurances concerning its benign impact could overcome the historical record, and a strike occurred centered on the manning of the automated machining centers.

At the opposite extreme, management at another plant not only secured employee acceptance of change but also through its public recognition of employee efforts encouraged whole-hearted employee support that made the transition successful. In its introduction of flexible manufacturing in an operation, management had set a goal of being in production by the first week in June. Although it reached that goal, the part produced did not work. Technical flaws dogged the project, and production remained below the quotas set until mid-November. By then, the technical problems were solved, and weekly production quotas always were exceeded after that.

Management established a program to express its appreciation to employees for their cooperation in solving the problems and reaching the production goals. Plaques were given to all personnel in the unit in recognition of their efforts. The achievement of particular milestones, such as the production of the millionth part, became occasions for expressing appreciation to the employees, with banners displayed commemorating the event. All employees involved, including the hourly ones, received a clock and a cup. For the managerial and technical employees, there was a special appreciation dinner in addition. Management labels its program as one of "Credibility, Communication, and Recognition." Its behavior toward the employees in this unit, moreover, has made employees in other units undergoing technological change much more accepting of it.

Attitudes toward innovation varied among employee groups. The greatest distinction was in length of service, with short-service employees the most flexible and accepting of new technology. That attitudes deteriorated with years of service is not a totally unexpected finding, for the longer an individual has been doing a job in a particular way, the more reluctant he or she is to switch to an entirely new way of operating.

To a considerable degree, these variances in reaction to new technology appear to be differences by age, with older employees being the least adaptable. Actually it is not age that is the determining factor but length of service. Of course, length of service itself is correlated with age, but a 35 year old who has been in a plant for seventeen years performing work in one way is as reluctant to change as a 55 year old with as many years of service.

The matter of age and length of service was a formidable problem for many operations and helps to explain the bias in favor of early retirement rather than layoff of younger employees when job cutbacks are necessary. At one plant, management and union officials agreed that older workers have grave problems of adapting to new technology. When one process, with a preponderance of employees in their fifties, was automated, half the operators opted for early retirement; most of the rest, rather than undergo retraining, exercised their seniority to move to other assignments.

Generalizations concerning any group of workers, including long-service ones, however, mask great variations within groups. Many older and high-seniority employees are quite pleased to work with new technology. In conversation, an older worker who had been a welder all his working life but was now operating a robot welder expressed great enthusiasm about the change, and he showed us how the robot performs a better weld than a human can.

Employee attitudes toward change, moreover, affect all types of change, not only technological. For example, moving to a sociotechnical approach to work organization, with autonomous teams directing their own activities, requires as much redirection of employee thinking and ways of operating as new technology. Companies operating sociotechnical systems, thus, must adopt specific selection criteria, particularly the ability to function in a group atmosphere, and not all employees are equally adaptable. Unionized operations shifting to sociotechnical systems may have even greater problems in changing worker attitudes, since traditional job structures and ways of relating between labor and management have been institutionalized through collective bargaining. These problems can be exacerbated when some units in a plant operate sociotechnically while others adhere to traditional systems.

Sometimes the impact of new technology on work flow also affects worker attitudes toward it. Under the old system at one plant manufacturing intricate electronic equipment for the aircraft industry, the operators and assemblers could judge how much work was available by the backlog of items awaiting them. Now the process is under computer control, and the work flows smoothly in a continuous stream. The employees, not seeing a backlog of items, believe that their work is running out, and so they tend to slow their efforts.

A test center supervisor said that after computerization, almost all the test technicians resented losing control of what they work on, though they have access to the data base and can override the system. According to a process engineer, although there was no obvious resistance, there was an undercurrent of reluctance to use the system. Management's perceptions were borne out by an interview with a test technician. As he put it, he is "not into computers" but is trying to use the system effectively. He complained about the steady pace of work and not being able to work in spurts anymore and no longer being able to choose the item upon which to work. His primary discontent, however, was software-caused system breakdowns, which prevented the technicians from completing their work on schedule.

The IRC survey of opinions concerning computer-based technology found pessimism about first-level supervisors' willingness to accommodate change and saw great anxiety at the lower levels of management. These perceptions were largely confirmed by the empirical research. More negative reactions to new technology came from the managerial-supervisory group than from production workers. Given its strategic position within the organization, this group can often effectively block change. In most plants, about two-thirds of the first-line supervisors have risen from the production worker ranks, and they see computer-based technology as threatening their technical competence. With the advent of a more highly sophisticated work force and company practices of employee involvement, foremen also feel a loss of power.

Altered job classifications further confuse supervisors. Because the maintenance of computer-based technology involves new or mixed skills, management has been combining or creating new job classifications or, when this has not been possible, setting up teams with the needed mix. Many foremen, however, remain traditional skills oriented and either do not know how, or do not want, to supervise combined groups.

Even when supervisory personnel do not resist new technology, they do not look forward to it. Usually there is turmoil in the early stages of breaking in a new technology as it is debugged. The line manager is responsible for getting production out but is unable to maintain schedules due to equipment breakdowns.

It is particularly difficult to keep employees working efficiently on the old process during the transition while the best workers have been taken off to be trained for the new automated processes. The frustration of supervisors under these conditions is quite understandable. Nevertheless, although a minority of supervisors has not been able to make the transition, most have been retrained successfully. One company made specific efforts to foster supervisory acceptance of change. It initiated its employee involvement program with foremen and then brought production workers into it. The supervisors, for example, have been included in the task forces designing new technology, and then, as heads of their work teams, they help plan its implementation.

Of all members of the work force, technical employees are most receptive of new technology. Although some engineers over thirty are unfamiliar with, and therefore apprehensive about, the computer, the younger technical people are particularly fascinated with the intricacies of computer-based systems. Some have microcomputers at home and are happy to work with them on the job. Many come to work early and study the system on their own.

5
Training and Retraining

A majority of respondents to the IRC opinion survey believe that training and development will be the employee relations activity most affected by computer-based technology and that the need for continuous upgrading of skills will significantly expand the employee relations role. Most respondents also believe that displaced workers can be retrained for other jobs in the same company and that the primary responsibility for funding and conducting such training rests with industry itself.

Need for Training

The empirical findings substantiate these viewpoints; training is the key to successful implementation of computer-based technology. Japanese manufacturing workers receive more continuous training than those in the United States, and much of the success of the Japanese has been attributed to their stress on employee training and retraining. American manufacturers are learning that lesson; every company in the study emphasized the critical role of training for the successful operation of programmable automation.

The importance of the human input into the productive process has been known for many years. T. W. Schultz earned a Nobel Prize in economics for his pioneering work in this field.[1] The United States has invested vast sums in its human capital through public educational systems and company training and development programs. Our research indicates that these investments are paying off in the quality of the American industrial work force. Apprehensions about the competence of existing company work forces to operate new sophisticated technology efficiently were in almost all cases unfounded. Although workers had to be trained in the new processes, they were amenable to and for the most part capable of benefiting from such training.

For most companies, training workers for computer-based technologies presents few significant problems or departures. Training remains a normal line management function, for training is ongoing as product mixes change, technology is altered, and employees are advanced to higher-level positions. Most employees therefore are used to being retrained.

Companies are determined to train their current employees in the new skills required for a number of reasons. Company philosophies regarding their work forces are changing, and they are coming to regard them as valuable assets that are renewable through retraining in new skills. By investing in training, a company ensures itself a work force capable of efficiently operating new processes.

Management also desires to broaden the jobs that workers can perform, and this obviously must be accomplished by training them in additional skills. Workers are trained to perform more tasks so that they can diagnose and prevent malfunctions, and they also are taught problem-solving skills. Such training produces a more versatile work force that is more easily redeployed as technology and the organization of work continue to change.

Although training may be expensive, it is cheaper than any alternative. Hiring new workers is costly, and since the control skills emanating from computerized processes are themselves new, those newly hired would be no more likely to possess them than current employees. The latter, moreover, are familiar with company procedures, they know the product lines, and they know their fellow workers and managers.

Even if workers with the requisite skills were available in the labor market, companies still would retrain current employees because they feel an obligation to them. They have been loyal employees and are not responsible for changing job requirements; as long as they are amenable to being retrained, that is what companies do. One company plans to use training as a prime means of preventing layoffs. Although its program is still largely in the design stage, it would work in the following manner: if the work of a group of technicians were to disappear, the affected employees would be retrained to do part of the engineer's job. This program would both preserve jobs for the redundant technicians and free engineers for more professional tasks. If new technology eliminated the jobs of some production workers, they would be retrained to do lower technical jobs. The key to this program is a system of assessment, selection, and training to upgrade employee skills throughout the organization. For the technical personnel, there would be individual development plans, whereby each engineer or other professional would be given the resources to learn new skills through time off for study, university television courses in-house, and attendance at technical seminars.

Failure to train employees adequately can undermine efficient operations. Poorly trained workers make mistakes that result in parts rejects and the need for costly rework. Under automation, with its integration of production, worker errors can lead to a breakdown of the entire system and even to serious accidents. One company that was emphasizing training was motivated to do so largely because it ascribed a serious accident in a previous introduction of new technology to a lack of proper employee training.

Insufficient attention to training often leads to unanticipated problems, as exemplified by the experience of one plant that had introduced an entirely new process for manufacturing its product. Since the preparation for the introduction of the change took place when plant employment was down, only the existing work force was retrained. Management did not anticipate the speed and vigor of the resurgence in sales, and it found itself operating a second shift before it could get retraining for recalled workers underway. The original training had been conducted largely by the vendors of the new equipment, but their contractual training requirements had expired, forcing plant management into crash programs to train the recalled workers. This company learned some hard lessons from its experience:

1. Build training costs into budget requests for new projects.
2. Engage in in-house training rather than relying too heavily on vendors.
3. Make sure that the training is replicable so that additional workers can receive proper instruction in operating and controlling new equipment.

As the company prepared to automate the manufacturing process in another plant, $2.5 million was earmarked for training, and the first person hired was the training director.

Matching Jobs and Workers

The ability of U.S. workers to handle programmable automation does not mean that every worker can; problems arise when some are not retrainable.

All the companies reported that younger workers, whether production or professional, are more easily trained than older ones. Because they have been out of school a shorter time they are less fearful of a classroom environment. They are better educated and tend to adapt more readily to computerization, and because they have not been doing a job in a certain way for many years, they are not set in their ways. In fact, receptivity to training is becoming an important selection criterion in hiring, particularly for companies adhering to no-layoff policies.

A distinct problem in retraining is the reluctance of some workers to undergo it. At one plant, technological change was going to eliminate a few dozen jobs in a unit. Management provided long advance notice to the workers, largely older female assemblers, and offered them retraining for other comparably paid jobs in the plant. Most of the workers refused retraining, though the alternative might mean reduced compensation or even losing their jobs.

Retraining some workers may not be possible. A plant that converted its warehouse to ASRS found that the required maintenance skills rose significantly. The existing warehouse maintenance force not only had inadequate skills but was unsuitable for retraining. Since the existing work was unskilled, the group included a number of people with problems such as alcoholism. Under the new system, maintenance employees would have to be much more skilled and would have to work largely unsupervised, so management had to hire new employees for these jobs and transfer those displaced elsewhere in the plant. The problem was partly solved by keeping the warehouse maintenance crew to a minimum and calling on plant maintenance in the event of serious problems.

Management wants to choose the best workers for new processes, but this is not always possible. In unionized situations, seniority is often specified by the labor-management agreement. Even in nonunion plants, foremen tend to object to higher management's treating the members of their crews on other than an equal basis.

In one unionized facility in which automation led to job upgrading, the senior qualified individual requesting a position always got it. Management never tried to promote a less senior person, even when, in its judgment, that person had superior ability to perform the job. At the same time, no unqualified person was advanced, since ability must be proved by passing tests.

Management at another plant that is organized has been able to select appropriate people in an indirect way. Assignment of individuals to new jobs is based on posting, with seniority playing the major role in choosing among applicants. As required by the collective bargaining agreement, management takes all the bidders, but after a detailed explanation of the job, those people who are less interested or fearful about their ability to perform the work (often those with the greatest seniority) drop out voluntarily.

Companies are attempting to develop more sophisticated techniques for matching people and jobs in the hourly and salaried categories. More and more, people are needed who are able to read, comprehend, and act on their own. Not everyone in existing work forces meets these criteria. When one plant transferred formerly laid-off machinists to inventory control, management discovered that some of them could not count or read. (Complaints about reading and writing abilities of employees at all levels, from unskilled laborers to professional engineers, were voiced a number of times.)

In most cases, however, the introduction of new sophisticated technology has made management aware of the capabilities of company work forces. As a result, they have been able to expand the scope of jobs. This appraisal of employee competence has been a key factor in leading companies into programs of employee involvement and widened spans of control.

Training throughout the Organization

Production and Maintenance Workers

The new technology mandates retraining throughout the organization. In addition to the obvious need to train the production workers, retraining of maintenance workers is also required. Programmable automation encompasses many highly intricate machines and processes, so proper maintenance is essential. As a consequence, there is much more, and more complicated, work for maintenance employees. Because the newest technology involves electronics and computers, the current skills of maintenance employees are often not sufficient, and they require a great deal of additional training.

In view of the heightened technical requirements for maintaining computerized equipment, selection criteria for maintenance jobs have been upgraded. Even toolmakers need new skills—for example, working with end effector designs of robots. They have the capacity to learn the new skills, and automation managers believe that they are adaptive to the new technology and enjoy working with it. One company reported that its toolmakers had obtained more new patents than had its engineers.

In view of the problems of maintenance of sophisticated computerized equipment, many plants have enlarged production worker jobs to include preventive maintenance and have retrained workers accordingly. The urgent need for preventive maintenance was identified in one plant through its quality circles. The operators were trained successfully in maintenance and in programming the computerized machines. A plant introducing a flexible manufacturing system had a similar experience, but its management decided to do the training by stages rather than overwhelm the workers.

In discussions with engineering personnel, however, we were told that there are limits to the application of automated processes that are related to equipment maintenance. Processes cannot be too complicated for the work force to maintain. One company has trained its workers to do basic programming, but it doubts they can do much more. To this degree, the level of automation is limited by the ability of the personnel who must keep the processes operating efficiently.

With respect to production and maintenance workers, the only shortages reported were in the skilled trades. While most plants faced no shortages, some said that no craftsmen were available in their local labor markets, and thus they had to train their own. To that end, they operate apprenticeship training programs.

Supervisors and Other Salaried Personnel

One mistake companies have made is to concentrate training efforts on production and maintenance workers, to the neglect of salaried personnel. One company, when it introduced CAD, trained only those draftsmen who were to be involved immediately and failed to extend CAD training to the others once initial needs were met. As a result, it now finds itself with two classes of draftsmen: those who know how to operate under CAD and those who do not. The latter group will have to be retrained eventually because non-CAD work is disappearing.

Supervisory training is of paramount importance. Since so many supervisors have come up the ranks from production, they tend to be deficient in technical areas. Retraining also is needed to overcome deficiencies in interpersonal skills, which have become more important as a result of the moves toward employee involvement and the fact that the work force of the 1980s is very different from that of the past.

Nonetheless, many companies neglected the retraining of supervisors, complicating their steps toward new technology work organization. At one plant that operates with worker autonomy and teams, most of the supervisors remain Theory X oriented (assuming that employees dislike work and, therefore, must be coerced into performing it), which caused many difficulties. Today, however, a number of companies are investing heavily in such training. Some companies that now emphasize employee involvement also have successfully retrained their older "drill sergeant" supervisors for it. In fact, many of them, like converts to a new religion, have become the most militant advocates of the new approach.

Older supervisors who are set in their ways can sometimes present insuperable difficulties in retraining because of their negative attitudes. A facility that introduced seam and automatic welding equipment discovered that long-service supervisors were reluctant to use it, preferring the old methods. Management undertook to train them on the new equipment in hopes of overcoming their resistance. Even when they were trained, however, they remained averse to the change. The facility is now doing 60 percent of its welding with the automatic equipment, but the supervisors still do not like it. Finally, management decided to bring in young supervisors for automatic welding and leave the old-timers as supervisors of traditional welding. The problem is being mitigated by the fact that the older supervisors are gradually retiring, and their places are being taken by younger people who are more willing to operate with the new technology.

Engineers

In many facilities, professional engineers have been in special need of learning new ways. Many of them, out of school for a decade or more, have never even worked with computers, much less know anything about computer-based technology; they have become obsolete. Their companies are sending them back to school for course work in the new technologies. This need reinforces the view expressed by many managers that an industrial plant today must be located near a university.

A large number of companies, however, charge the engineering schools with failure to graduate engineers with computer knowledge and the ability to apply such knowledge. They also accuse the schools of neglecting human relations skills in their training. One company was adamant in its condemnation of engineering and business schools for their failure to teach students about the technological and organizational interrelationships so important with the advent of computer-based systems. The company charges that engineering graduates are ignorant of organizational and managerial matters, and business school graduates know little or nothing about manufacturing processes and changing technology. The result in industry is often a failure to mesh technological and organizational systems to achieve the highest potential efficiency.

The long gestation period of CIM has one major advantage: it will allow time for universities to alter their curricula to meet new technological needs and for the companies to retrain employees for the new technology. We are likely to see eventually not the "worker-less" factory, but the "production-worker-less" factory as that category of worker is upgraded to operator-maintenance employee.

Most of the reports of skill shortages related to engineering personnel, particularly those trained in CAD. Not only were the internal supplies of such engineers inadequate, but they were scarce in the external labor market as well. Given the dearth of engineers with the skills needed, many companies are developing those skills through internal training of their engineers. One company, in which new technology relates to the development of composites, faces an acute shortage of materials engineers; seeing no immediate solution, it has endowed chairs at engineering schools so that more people will be trained in the area for the longer term.

A company that was introducing a new technology found that it required new sets of engineering skills. Since engineers with such skills could not be found, it hired some new graduates and also retrained its current engineers. It discovered, however, that electrical engineers who have been out of school for ten or more years experience difficulty in making the transition to the application of computerized processes to manufacturing production.

The opposite problem sometimes arises with respect to top engineering talent: what to do with people who have been involved in the design of new processes once the project has been completed and another is not immediately at hand. Such individuals often are loathe to accept positions as engineers in the traditional environments of industrial plants. If no other outlets for their creativity exist at the moment, they are likely to move on to other companies where they can design advanced technology.

Management

Middle management also must be retrained, attitudinally as well as technically. The companies reported that the vast majority adapt; they must, or they lose their jobs because there are no collective bargaining clauses protecting them from dismissal. The pace of change so far, however, has been moderate enough not to cause undue stress in middle management ranks.

With managerial as well as technical personnel, human relations abilities are sometimes a problem, particularly since computer-based technology requires more interaction among employees—managerial, technical, maintenance, and production. One company has adopted a formal policy of not promoting even the best technical people if they do not have the requisite human relations skills. It is not easy to evaluate such skills, and the human resource function operates as a partner with line management on all promotions. Conversations are held with the union, too, on the kinds of persons it wants as managers.

Senior management also is affected by computer-based technology, for it must envision a new industrial order. If senior managers stick to the traditional short-term horizons, their companies will not be able to move ahead. Advanced technology causes immense changes in the ways products are designed, made, and sold—in fact, in the entire way business operates. Some senior managers therefore try to avoid the problems associated with change by moving into new technology hesitantly. Necessity, however, has overcome hesitancy in most cases and certainly in most of the companies in the study.

Most companies are beginning to pay much more attention to management training, both internal and external. Programs run by the companies themselves cover training from first-level supervision through department head. There also are external management development programs to which managers, particularly senior ones, are sent. One company budgets $700 per manager for outside training costs, and another requires every manager, at every level, to take at least forty hours of training each year.

Designing Training Programs

The need for interaction among the human resources function, engineering, and manufacturing is crucial if employees are to be able to operate new technology efficiently. Training programs cannot be devised until the jobs for which people will be retrained are identified and their skill requirements delineated. This is not necessarily easy because the jobs must be analyzed during the period in which the technology is being developed, and not everything is clearly understood yet.

The next problem is finding trainers. This task is especially troublesome when the change is a facility's first venture into computerized manufacturing, and its own employees, including its engineers, are not yet familiar with the processes. The difficulties help to explain the heavy dependence on vendors for initial training. Relying on vendors, however, has drawbacks: the training they provide is often superficial, they are unfamiliar with the culture of a facility and may encounter human relations problems, and they have no responsibility for continuity in training. Thus a plant must develop its own training abilities and programs as quickly as possible.

Reliance on Vendors versus In-House Training

The danger of overreliance on vendors was dramatized at one facility visited. Interviews with workers on the shop floor revealed a good deal of unhappiness with the new technology, particularly its frequent breakdowns, which were attributed partly to its design but mostly to the meagerness of formal training programs. The plant depends almost exclusively on vendors for the training on new equipment, but this program does not always work well. For example, a utility worker was supposed to be trained for the automated equipment by an engineer from the vendor, but he was in a hurry and touched only on the highlights, and because he spoke with a heavy foreign accent, she barely understood the few instructions he did give her. She had, in effect, taught herself how to operate the equipment by studying the manuals and came to understand the machine's operation through day-to-day use. Since other workers received even less training than she had, she trains them, on her own, in the use of the machine. This training is done informally; coworkers come to her as a resource whenever they need help.

This instance, rather than being a worst case, at least involved direct training, even if it was superficial. In other new installations at that plant, only engineers are trained by the vendors, and then the engineers show the operators how to run the machines. Since the engineers are themselves not trained as trainers, they often are poor teachers; they tend to assume a level of worker knowledge that is unrealistic. As a result, the workers do not properly understand the operation of new computerized machines, which leads to system breakdowns. Even the supervisors are not given sufficient technical training.

Corporate headquarters confirmed that training is the company's biggest weakness in the area of new technology, and top management has come to recognize, albeit belatedly, that effective training is vital. Two steps are being taken to correct the situation. First, the company is including money for training in its budgets for all new technological installations. Second, the personnel department, which oversees training, is to work with engineering and with line departments to prepare its own in-house training programs. This new emphasis on training will take time to implement, however.

At another company, which has a central robotics laboratory at headquarters, the laboratory does the development work for the installation of a robot. Once that robot is in place at a plant, line management takes over. The same relationship exists with the training required; the laboratory is responsible for the initial training of supervisors and the top operator, but the plant must train all the other people who will be involved, directly or indirectly, with the robot's operation and maintenance.

Given the increased training needs, one facility recently shifted to centralization of all training. A systems and training group was established to anticipate the needs flowing from new technology. The group interacts with engineering. In the past, greater reliance had been placed on vendors of new equipment for training, as was done in the cases of both CAD and NC machines, but now the facility conducts most of its own training.

Cooperation with Local Educational Institutions

In addition to in-house training and training by vendors of automated equipment, educational institutions—technical schools and colleges and universities—are becoming an indispensable resource for employers. As management assumes a larger responsibility for training employees in specific skills for operating, maintaining, and servicing technology, local educational institutions are being used to raise the general educational and skill levels of the work force. Many managements have come to the conclusion that, because of computer-based technology, proximity to a university is a requirement in plant location.

At one plant, both the management and the union have recognized that mental work is replacing physical labor in the workplace and the employees must be equipped with the skills to meet this challenge. Plant management arranged with a local state-run vocational school to teach classes in reading, mathematics, and computer skills. About 400 employees (20 percent of the plant's work force) were enrolled in some course at the time of our visit. Funding for this training is provided in part by a company–national union training fund established through collective bargaining.

In addition, management established its own on-site training center to facilitate skill upgrading, particularly of tradesmen. Employees are taught computer skills and related subjects by management personnel and by their peers. Peer training was found to be extremely effective. Employees are able to study on their own with computer training modules or in classroom settings. Using computers in training can be extremely effective because employees get immediate feedback on what they are doing right or wrong.

Worker reaction to the training appeared to be favorable. A utility painter, who was now operating robotic spray painting, reported that he had not been anxious about his ability to learn to use the new technology. With twenty-six hours of classroom study, supplemented by on-the-job training, he was able to program robots, make minor repairs, and operate the computer console. Although he did not understand all the technical aspects of the computer, he felt comfortable operating it because it is user friendly.

Although his direct responsibility is only the painting robots, he has to be aware of the entire painting process because the various components are linked in a system.

A local community college assisted in retraining for the conversion of a warehouse to automated storage and retrieval. The company contacted the college, which tested the workers for ability to be retrained; only 10 percent of them achieved the minimum score that the college itself required for admittance to its programs. The difficulties were isolated—very poor language and computational abilities within the warehouse work force—and highlighted the need for a great deal of remedial work. Remediation was provided to those with the greatest potential. It was successful in improving the workers' mathematical abilities but less so with respect to language, since Spanish was the first language of many of them.

The retraining was carried out under the state of California's apprenticeship program and with company personnel acting as instructors. Initially the trainees received eighty hours of classroom instruction in basic computer theory and in operating the equipment. Once the initial group was trained, all subsequent training of new ASRS workers has been done by management in-house, and the classroom instruction time has been reduced to forty hours because there no longer is a remediation problem (only qualified employees are now transferred to the ASRS). Moreover, more of the training now is on the job.

This plant's experience in converting a warehouse to ASRS, which could have led to the termination of a group of employees, turned out well for everyone. With remediation, formerly unskilled workers were successfully trained to operate an automated warehouse. One person presented a fascinating case. She could hardly speak English and even now cannot conduct a conversation in it, but she is one of the best workers in the warehouse, having learned enough English to interact well with the computer. The trained workers, moreover, have been upgraded to much more highly paid positions, receiving increases in pay of up to one-third. Those who could not qualify for the remediation have been transferred to other unskilled jobs in the plant.

Other states, particularly in the South, have also been active in employee training. At a plant in South Carolina, hiring of employees is a cooperative effort between the company and the state. Plant management interviews and conducts the initial selection of potential hirees, but they have to complete the state-provided training course successfully before they become company employees.

Another facility, which is basically a skilled craftsman operation, needs to increase its employees' skills so they can operate more complicated machinery. With no skilled workers available in its local labor market, the facility must train its own, and to that end, it operates its own apprentice school. Enrollment is 900, and the students are trained in twenty trades common to the industry. The apprenticeship school is an accredited one; it is a four-year program that can be completed in thirty-four months. Eighty percent of the enrollees come from outside the area, but they are required to work for the company upon graduation. Fifty percent of the company's supervisors have come from those trained in an apprenticeship, and 85 percent of the graduates are now supervisors.

Thoughts on Training

A number of lessons with respect to training for computer-based technology are apparent:

1. Because computer-based technology eliminates some jobs, creates new ones, and changes the requirements of others, training is essential for employees at all levels. Training of supervisors and managers is at least as important as training of production and maintenance workers.
2. Training and retraining needs must be anticipated and their cost built into the investment budgets of projects. Otherwise funds adequate for the level of instruction required may not be available.
3. To forecast training needs accurately, human resources must work closely with engineering and manufacturing to determine future job requirements.
4. To the degree possible, training should be conducted in-house to avoid overreliance on vendors.
5. Training should be replicable, so new or transferred employees can receive proper instruction in operating and controlling new equipment.
6. New training techniques, including the use of the computer itself and peer training, are particularly effective.
7. If a company is moving toward greater employee involvement and autonomy, special training in this area is essential. Training is especially needed by supervisors, who must become team leaders rather than production pushers.
8. The local educational community can be an important resource. Many states provide training assistance. Universities can provide general education and human relations training while the company provides specific and technical training.
9. Companies should recognize that the programmable automation revolution is a continuous one and that training is an ongoing process, with the skills of the work force constantly upgraded to match the requirements of ever-advancing technology.

6
The Employment Effects of Computer-based Technology

Most of the U.S. experts surveyed by IRC did not see significant job displacements traceable to robotics occurring within the next few years. Almost two-thirds of those respondents disagreed with the statement that 10 million to 15 million manufacturing workers would be displaced from their jobs during the mid-to late 1980s because of technological change and foreign production.[1] Although some displacement will result from technology, the respondents anticipated that its effects can be managed given the long lead time required to bring sophisticated forms of automation on-line. Although some displaced workers will need to relocate, transfer to new fields, or accept lower-paying jobs, the overwhelming majority of experts believes that most displaced workers can be reemployed within their own company.

Complexity of Problems Besetting Industries

Our hopes of isolating the employment effects of new technology were quickly dashed. In the past half-dozen years, the United States has experienced two back-to-back recessions (that in 1981–1982 of major proportions), demand for many American products has been in decline, and imports have flooded U.S. markets. Under these conditions, it is not possible to determine whether reduced levels of employment in a plant are due to one or more of these factors or to the introduction of new technology. Reduced employment, moreover, may not necessarily mean that workers were laid off, for in many instances, companies have used attrition to trim the work force.

Another reason for our inability to isolate employment effects of new technology is the multiplant, multiproduct nature of many of the companies studied. First, companies tend to introduce new technology in the manufacture of new or growing product lines, and, as a result of increased production volume, any displacements that occur can be absorbed. Second, these companies have the ability to move products among plants, so if new technology threatens a reduction in personnel requirements at one plant, another product can be transferred in.

Furthermore, what seems like a large impact on employment within a specific unit may be much smaller when viewed within an entire plant and even inconsequential when seen within the perspective of an entire company. One company reported employment reductions in some of its plants caused by market conditions but none by new technology. Part of the reason is the slow pace of innovation. The head of its robotics laboratory stated, "In a company with more than 100,000 employees, seventeen robots cannot have much impact." The company has introduced more than robots; nevertheless, it has not had to let go a single worker as a result.

Ten of the sixteen companies (or the divisions) studied have experienced declines in employment in the past half-dozen years related to macroeconomic factors, not technological change. Among those ten, seven were subject to increased competition from imports, and four of them also experienced some decline in product market demand. In two cases, the overwhelming explanation for the loss of jobs was decline in the product market. Only in the one remaining case could the failure of employment to recover its pre-1981—1982 recession level be attributed to improved productivity; although employment went up, it did not go up as much as the increase in production. Absent the new technology, however, the company's share of the product market might have been considerably lower, and so might have been its employment.

The overwhelming motive for introducing computer-based technology was to restore competitiveness. Many of the companies, however, even with the new technology, were still having difficulty competing with foreign producers, largely because the higher value of the U.S. dollar in the mid-1980s, which made American products relatively more expensive, undercut their efforts. While consumers and business have been buying more manufactured goods, much of the increase has benefited imports, thus cutting sales, production, and jobs for Americans. (Even the late 1987 decline in the dollar's value has been of only modest help because much of the competition comes from products manufacured in countries that tie the value of their own currencies to the dollar, such as Taiwan and Korea.)

Since innovation increases efficiency, there is no question that in the absence of increased production, employment drops as a result of new technology; that is simply a truism. The complicated interaction among product market demand, competition, both foreign and domestic, and technology can be illustrated by the experience of the operations visited.

A plant that came close to operating with CIM opened in 1978, and its advanced technology made it very efficient. As a result, its volume of production increased, and so did its production worker employment, which reached 755 in 1982. That level represented a peak; the market for one of its two products began to deteriorate. (The domestic industry that used the product was declining because of a loss of markets to imports, making this plant an indirect victim of foreign competition.) As the production processes have been continually improved, the increased efficiency, combined with stable or even slightly declining output, led to a reduction in jobs. Employment dropped to 715 in 1983, 679 in 1984, and 643 in 1985, by which point it was below the plant's initial employment. Further declines were in store, and management estimated that if there was no resurgence in demand for the product, production workers' jobs would drop to 614 in 1986 and 590 in 1987.

Next consider a plant producing electronic control devices. With product demand growing slowly, each competing firm strives for some advantage. This company's major competitors sought that advantage by relocating their operations either to low-wage southern areas or offshore. The traditional method of manufacture was hand assembly, and this company now found itself at a tremendous labor cost disadvantage. In searching for a solution, it decided that it wanted to maintain production in its existing location in a midwestern city. To do so, however, it would have to introduce new technology that would lead to greater efficiency in production.

The product was redesigned to reduce its labor content and to permit automated production. The manual assembly line was replaced with a computer-controlled assembly operation, which incorporated robot transfer agents, torque-regulated screw driving stations, and on-line quality control, including a vision system to ensure that the product was positioned correctly as it moved along the line. The product is now 100 percent computer inspected for calibration.

In order to minimize effects on employees, the company follows a strategy of trying to introduce the new technology during the upward phase of the business cycle. In this case, its timing was perfect, for the new automated line was introduced in the summer of 1982, just as the nation began to pull out of the recession. Although automation of the production line did lead to displacement, employees could be transferred to other jobs, pursuant to the provisions of the collective bargaining agreement.

The experience of this company can be interpreted in two ways. The first focuses on the fact that the new technology led to a reduction of jobs in this operation. Total employment in the unit dropped by 25, or 3.8 percent, from its initial 650. That only 25 workers had to be taken out of the unit is attributable to the improvement in business stemming from a combination of national economic recovery and the greater efficiency afforded by automation, which increased the company's competitive position in the product market. The second view recognizes that had the new manufacturing process not been introduced, the entire operation could not have continued at that location. The employees and the union espoused the second view and cooperated with management in making the new automated line successful. The fact that no one had to be laid off was most important in gaining that acceptance.

A manufacturer of communications equipment found itself in a similar predicament as cheaper products from Taiwan eroded its product market, causing the layoff of 900 workers. It explained to its employees and to the union representing the production and maintenance workers that the imports threatened its survival in that product market unless it improved efficiency. The union did not regret its decision to cooperate since the increased sales that followed the introduction of a redesigned product and new automated methods of production led to recall of 500 of the laid-off workers. Clearly this is a case in which new technology created, rather than destroyed, jobs.

A plant producing bearings also found itself in trouble. The problems of the entire industry are analyzed in a recent report, *Competitive Assessment of the U.S. Ball and Roller Bearing Industry*, prepared by the International Trade Commission at the behest of Congress. Connecticut, the leading production state, has seen its ball bearings industry employment decline by 50 percent, from 16,000 in the mid- to late 1960s to about 7,600 in the mid-1980s. Exports declined, and imports rose rapidly. The trade problem, "combined with increased automation, a depressed market for bearings and a restructuring in the industry to reduce labor-intensive processes, helped reduce employment in the first half of the [1980s] decade."[2]

The plant we visited was a typical batch operation, producing bearings of various sizes in small lots. Three NC machines with robot arms for loading were introduced. Jobs in that operation were reduced because one person rather than three now could run the machining center. With two-shift operation, there was a net decline of four jobs.

The greatest benefit of the machining center, however, was not labor savings, but reduced setup time when a different sized bearing was to be machined. Resetting the old automatic screw machines had required an average of thirty hours, but the CNCs needed only a half-hour of reprogramming. Management hopes that the greater flexibililty will enable the plant to become more competitive and increase its sales. If those hopes are realized, the new technology could lead to an enlargement in the plant work force that would more than compensate for the four jobs eliminated.

The need to put the employment impact of new technology in the perspective of the larger economic environment also can be seen in the experience of a steel company. In the past decade, the U.S. steel industry has been doubly hit—by declining demand for its products and by imports taking a greater share of the smaller market. Since 1980, U.S. employment in blast furnaces has dropped 45 percent, from 512,000 to 280,000. The company we visited has done relatively well, suffering only a 37.5 percent decline in employment.

The company was in the process of introducing a state-of-the-art continuous casting process run with a multilevel computer system. This will result in the loss of about 360 jobs, a small number when compared with the thousands of jobs lost since 1980. Indeed the whole purpose in adopting the new technology is to increase the company's efficiency and competitiveness in order to stem the decline in production and, hence, in employment. If successful, technological change will save many more jobs than it eliminates.

Positive Role of Innovation

Innovation thus can play a positive role in job preservation and enhancement, even when the data would seem to indicate just the opposite. This positive impact can be seen in the experience of an electrical manufacturer. This plant produces a consumer good that in 1982 underwent significant change in design, as well as in manufacturing process. With the introduction of programmable automation, employment in the plant declined from 1,612 in January 1981 to 1,513 by late 1984, as a one-quarter rise in productivity outstripped a one-sixth increase in production.

Employment, however, had dropped dramatically with the onset of the 1981–1982 recession, which occurred before the design and technological changes were introduced. In 1983, production rose with the economic recovery, and faster than the company had anticipated, because the redesigned product had garnered a greater share of its market. As a result, employment jumped back up, and a second shift had to be resumed, which led to the recall of all laid-off workers. In this case, innovation undoubtedly had increased employment. Had the product and its process of manufacture not changed, the company's market share would not have increased, and employment would have remained closer to its recession level than to that achieved in 1984.

This case illustrates the dilemma that society faces with respect to technology and employment. When product markets are no longer growing rapidly or are declining, employment seems to be negatively affected, no matter what a company does. If it fails to introduce new technology, it loses sales, and jobs disappear; if it modernizes sufficiently to preserve or even enlarge its markets, the increased efficiency reduces manpower requirements. Displacement, however, may not result, for the manpower reduction is usually small enough to be accomplished through normal attrition.

The positive role of technology can be seen in another plant that produces products for the railroad industry. The plant had been busy a few years before as the railroad industry was modernizing its equipment, but when that modernization program was completed, demand dropped sharply. As a result, plant employment is down almost 50 percent, from more than 2,000 to just over 1,000.

In an attempt to move into another, more sophisticated product line, the company introduced four computerized machining cells. No direct displacement was connected with the machining centers because they were related to the new product line. It was calculated that had they been placed in the old product line, their direct displacement impact would have been on the order of eight to one; close to fifty jobs would have been affected.

The employment impact of the new technology can be extended beyond direct displacements. The quality-control capabilities represented by the CNCs diminish the need for quality-control personnel. Fewer materials handlers are needed because tools and fixtures are for the most part automatically delivered to the machine. Offsetting the displacements to some degree are the technical and maintenance jobs created.

The new technology has not caused employment loss to the plant but has helped to keep its current employment. With the new capabilities afforded by the CNC machining centers, the company was able to bid on and secure a lucrative contract from a company in an industry outside its prime market. According to the vice-president of manufacturing, without that contract, the entire plant would have been closed. He also said that the principal benefit of the CNCs was not their labor cost savings, as great as they were, but rather their flexibility, which made possible the production of a large variety of different items, none of which had long runs.

Cases of Employment Increase

In the few cases in which output increased significantly because of increased product demand, employment also rose, despite technological change. This outcome was most common with facilities producing defense items. Some of them were hiring and training large numbers of new employees.

Growth in employment, however, was not limited to defense contractors. A company producing for the civilian airline industry was introducing an automated machining center. That center will eliminate eight or nine people at the existing level of production, but because the market is expanding, the company anticipates that the unit's employment actually will rise by a hundred within a year. Labor cost savings were not the objective of introducing the new technology, since direct labor cost is equal to only about 10 percent of the product selling price. The biggest savings sought are in materials through reductions in scrap and improvements in product quality.

A plant producing communications equipment was doubly blessed: with a growing market and with its ability to capture a greater share of that market, to which new technology made an important contribution. The plant uses all types of programmable automation, but let us focus on the automation of card production. The principles of the line card module were to develop a pull-through rather than a push-through production process; to remove as much human handling as possible, mainly to improve quality but also to save on labor; and to create a closed-loop computerized manufacturing system.

Originally 160 people worked in the card operation. With the new system, productivity has been increased fourfold. Even so, there are now 700 people in the operation, for, by 1985, production was ten times higher because the company had captured 40 percent of the market for the finished product. This increase was achieved partly through lower production costs but primarily through the increased quality and reliability of the product, which must function flawlessly for many years lest the communications networks of entire cities break down.

Impact on Women, Minorities, and Young Workers

In the IRC opinion survey, 60 percent of respondents indicated that they believed the new technology would encroach on jobs traditionally held by minorities and women. Research, however, revealed only limited evidence that minorities and women suffer disproportionately from employment reductions stemming from new technology. This can be explained in part by the fact that equal employment laws are now more than two decades old. Furthermore, most of the companies in the study had been hiring significant numbers of minorities and women long before the enactment of those laws because of the nature of their work and the state of the labor market. The automobile industry, for example, has been hiring blacks for many many decades because of its need for labor. Similarly, electrical and electronic plants, with large numbers of light assembly jobs, have always found women a prime source of labor. Thus blacks and women are as much protected by seniority as white males.

One case where there was a disproportionate impact on minority workers was a large plant in southern California that converted its warehouse to an ASRS. Most jobs in the warehouse had been of the low-skill materials-handling type, and, given the plant's location, the work force was composed largely of Mexican-Americans and some blacks. Before the introduction of ASRS, warehouse employment was 142; after, it was only 38. The jobs that remained were more complex and required computer skills. A disproportionate number of Mexican-Americans and blacks failed the qualifying test for retraining because of poor language and computational skills. Although remedial work eventually qualified some of them, the minority percentage of the ASRS work force was lower than that of the original warehouse. There was, however, no change in the ethnic composition of the total plant work force because those displaced from the warehouse were transferred to other unskilled jobs.

At a plant that had suffered a severe reduction in employment, the cutbacks had a disparate effect on the female work force. A decade ago, the plant work force was about 5,000; it is now less than 2,500. The greatest portion of the reduction was due to a decline in business, but the more recent reductions stem from a redesign of products to reduce their labor content and productivity improvements resulting from new technology. The new technology mainly affected assembler jobs, and since the assemblers were 90 percent female, the female proportion of the work force dropped from 49.5 percent in 1979 to 45.1 percent in 1985. Similarly the minority (black, Hispanic, and Asian) percentage dropped from 3.6 to 2.1.

If any group has been disproportionately affected by reduction in employment from whatever cause, it has been young workers, no matter what their sex or race. Manufacturing has not been an area of employment opportunity in recent years. In the plant just discussed, for example, the employment reductions have been so severe that twenty-one years of seniority is the average in the bargaining unit, and the average age of the work force is 46.5 years. This plant is getting to the end of its recall list since so many workers opted for early retirement or lost their recall rights, which are good only for three years. At the point of our visit, there were still 500 workers with recall rights, but between continued attrition and a resurgence in business, the plant anticipated beginning to hire again within a year, providing some jobs for younger people in the community and bringing down the average age and length of service of the work force.

Changed Composition of the Labor Force

New technology does not affect all types of jobs equally, with the consequence that the composition of the manufacturing work force is changing. In line with historic trends, indirect labor is growing relative to direct, and within the blue-collar ranks, maintenance is growing relative to production. Some traditional blue-collar jobs are disappearing. These are primarily lower-skilled jobs such as materials handling, plus some others such as spray painting and many types of welding. In some cases, jobs operating machines are declining in number, as are those involved in such assembly operations as placing or soldering. With more control built into computer-generated processes, some plants also report less need for quality-control inspectors. The greater stress on product reliability, however, led others to report a growth in testing and quality assurance jobs.

Computer-based technologies at the same time increase the number of employees in other types of jobs. Professional and technical jobs are increasing in numbers, particularly those associated with programming and maintaining equipment. One plant added an entire new unit, CAM Systems Engineering, which is responsible for high-level maintenance of the factory system, software maintenance, and opportunities for systems enhancement. A shortage of engineers familiar with computer-based technology was reported almost universally. Maintenance grows in importance but the skills needed now, however, are not necessarily those of traditional crafts. One company is retraining all its electricians to become electronic technicians, and others have found it necessary to combine mechanical and electrical skills.

The disparate impact on direct production work is most vividly illustrated by the experience of a plant manufacturing electronic control devices for aircraft (table 6–1). A combination of market deterioration and new technology over six years has slashed the plant work force by 37.8 percent, with much of the loss concentrated in the production and maintenance group, which declined 44 percent. With that magnitude of decline in the production unit, the need for supervisory employees also dropped, so management ranks within the plant decreased but only by 13.6 percent. Examination of the entire division of the company, which is located at this site, shows that some of the direct manufacturing job loss has been compensated for by an expansion of employment in marketing, engineering, finance, business development, and materials purchasing. As a result, the nonmanufacturing employment rose from one-third to more than one-half of the division's total employment.

This is an extreme case, however, and not typical with respect to the sharp decline of blue-collar jobs, which in most instances has been much more moderate. For the electrical plant in which employment dropped 6.1 percent, the entire reduction was in production workers, while maintenance and salaried employment rose (table 6–2). Within the bargaining unit, the direct-indirect labor ratio rose as a consequence from .24 to .29. The salaried-to-hourly employee ratio rose from 0.98 to 1.16.

Table 6–1
Employment Changes in Electronic Instrument Plant, before and after Introduction of New Technology

Job Category	April 1979 Number	April 1979 Percentage	April 1985 Number	April 1985 Percentage	Change Number	Change Percentage
Production-maintenance	951	86.9	533	78.4	−418	−44.0
Professional-technical	42	3.8	49	7.2	+7	+16.6
Management	59	5.4	51	7.5	−8	−13.6
Clerical	42	3.8	47	6.9	+5	+11.9
Total	1,094	100.0	680	100.0	−414	−37.8

Table 6–2
Employment Changes in Electrical Products Plant, before and after Introduction of New Technology

Job Category	January 1981 Number	January 1981 Percentage	January 1984 Number	January 1984 Percentage	Change Number	Change Percentage
Production	1,184	73.4	1,050	69.4	– 134	– 11.3
Maintenance	284	17.6	306	20.2	+ 22	+ 7.7
Subtotal	1,468	91.1	1,356	89.6	– 112	– 7.6
Professional-technical-management-clerical	144	8.9	157	10.4	+ 13	+ 19.0
Total	1,612	100.0	1,513	100.0	– 99	– 6.1

Despite the drop in the number of direct production workers, the plant's labor force is still overwhelmingly blue collar: 89.6 percent (it was 91.1 percent before the change). (Similarly employment in a plant in the transportation equipment industry, which has introduced many robots as well as computer-controlled systems, is still 82.5 percent blue collar.)

Thus although we find a relative decline of direct production work, and in some instances an absolute drop as well, it is not disappearing. Within production and maintenance units, the types of blue-collar jobs that are disappearing tend to be lower-skill ones. The impact on the blue-collar work force of a particular plant, however, will depend on both the nature of the product and the nature of the new technology.

In the division manufacturing electronic control devices for aircraft, for example, the sharpest declines were in the higher-paying jobs. To stem its market loss, the division introduced all types of computer-based technology, including automatic soldering and washing equipment, robots for materials handling, and an automated test center. The last had the effect of eliminating many high-skilled testing and control jobs (table 6–3). Grade 10 jobs, the highest in the bargaining unit, were virtually eliminated, while the bulk of jobs were downgraded from grades 6, 7, and 8, to grades 3, 4, and 5. The median job grade, as a result, fell from 7.51 to 5.15. In this case, new technology clearly downgraded the blue-collar work force.

This case, however, was atypical, for new technology usually leads to some, and occasionally to dramatic, upgrading. This occurs when workers, particularly operators, are upskilled through enlarged job duties, including problem solving and setup work. In one plant in an operation that had been converted to flexible manufacturing, there was substantial upgrading of direct labor (table 6–4). In this case, it was the lowest-level assembler jobs

Table 6–3
Distribution of Employment within the Bargaining Unit, by Job Grade, Division Manufacturing Electronic Control Device for Aircraft

	1979		1985	
Job Grade	Number	Percentage	Number	Percentage
10	569	11.6	18	0.8
9	398	8.1	184	8.2
8	987	20.0	297	13.3
7	1,034	21.0	160	7.1
6	589	12.0	192	8.6
5	477	9.7	313	14.0
4	351	7.1	447	20.0
3	440	8.9	591	26.4
2	79	1.6	36	1.6
Total	4,924	100.0	2,238	100.0

Table 6–4
Change in Distribution of Employment in Plant Unit Converted to a Flexible Manufacturing System

		Before Change		After Change	
Job Grade	Job	Number	Percentage	Number	Percentage
5	Troubleshooter, test technician	35	10.3	65	13.7
4	Machine operator, repairer, inspector	64	48.1	383	80.8
2 and 3	Assembler	142	41.6	26	5.5
Total		341	100.0	474	100.0

that were virtually eliminated by the new technology, while there was very sharp increase in higher-level operator, repairer, and inspector jobs, and a lesser increase in the still higher-level troubleshooter and test technician jobs.

The IRC opinion survey revealed that a majority of respondents believe that the new technology is leading to a skill twist, that is, eliminating semi-skilled jobs while creating jobs requiring significant technical knowledge. The fear emanating from this development is that large numbers of those who are displaced will be unable to qualify for the newly created jobs. Although research does indicate that some skill twist is taking place, workers are being retrained to meet the new requirements, and the vast majority of workers are able to upgrade their skills to qualify for available production jobs.

Short-Term Employment Outlook

It appears that for the next few years, many sectors of American manufacturing will not have new job opportunities for production workers. A number of companies stated unequivocally that the shaky state of the markets for many of their products, combined with the introduction of new technology, had resulted in little hiring of production workers. These companies expect this situation to continue, and some believe that even further labor displacement will take place, although all hope to avoid it by using attrition to trim the work force.

Product design may play as important a role as new equipment and processes in the declining need for production workers. Companies are trying to design labor out of their products in order to compete with imports from low-wage, less-developed countries. In addition, automation often acts as a catalyst for other moves toward greater efficiency in the utilization of labor.

That the introduction of new technology leads to labor displacement is not unexpected. In fact, if that were not to happen, automation would be a failure. As we know from economic theory, labor and capital are substitutes for each other to some extent, and employers can use different proportions of each to obtain an output. In practice, employers will choose the combination of labor and capital that costs the least. As the price of one goes up relative to the other, they will substitute more of the cheaper one. Thus as the price of labor has risen over time, more and more capital has been substituted for it. New capital investment, moreover, tends to embody the latest technology. New technology, in turn, alters the production function (the combination of labor and capital); that is, it makes it possible to obtain more output per unit of labor and capital. The new computer-based technologies are doing just that.

Technology has been an important source of much of the national economic growth[3] and underlies rising living standards. While there is nothing new in the phenomenon of substituting capital for labor, its impact today is different for many of the companies studied. Their product markets are no longer growing or are growing only modestly, so production is not increasing fast enough to avoid drops in employment.

To a large degree, these employment effects of technology have been influenced by the 1984–1985 time period in which the study was conducted. On the one hand, these were years of recovery from the worst post–World War II recession in which unemployment hit postwar highs. Most facilities in the study, moreover, were in industries heavily affected by the economic decline. Since much of the implementation of computer-based technologies occurred during this period of economic growth, negative impacts on unemployment were somewhat minimized.

Manufacturing—along with the other goods-producing sectors of the economy, agriculture and mining—did not benefit from the recovery as much as did other economic sectors. The entire world was in recession in the early 1980s, but high U.S. growth in 1983 and 1984 served to pull the rest of the world out of the doldrums. This was accomplished primarily by the other nations selling manufactured goods in the American market. The appreciation in the value of the U.S. dollar relative to other nations' currencies allowed foreign-produced goods to be priced lower than domestic goods, thus cutting American exports and increasing imports into the country. With foreign goods cheaper and American goods more expensive, the United States had a continually worsening trade deficit.

Exports of manufactured goods kept on slipping, and the United States, the world's leading industrial nation, became a net importer of manufactured goods. The trade picture has been reflected in employment statistics. Thus, many companies we visited were suffering greatly from foreign competition, which was affecting negatively their employment levels.

Sluggishness in the world economy has also contributed to the problems of American manufacturing. More robust world economic growth would expand the markets for manufactured goods, and faster growth within the economies of U.S. trading partners would mean that they could sell more of their production at home and not have to depend as much on exports to the United States. Their growing markets in turn would enable American goods to be exported to them.

When the world economy resumes a more balanced growth path, the new computer-based technologies being installed in American manufacturing will be the basis for increased output and employment. Making manufacturing more efficient, they will make it more competitive and thus able to provide more jobs. By late 1987, with the decline in the value of the U.S. dollar, U.S. exports of manufactured goods were growing, as was employment in manufacturing. For the long run, however, manufacturing is unlikely to provide an increasing number of jobs, because its output will not grow faster than its productivity improvement.

7
Dealing with Displacement

In the 1960s, the major human resource problems confronting most, if not all, of the companies in the IRC study of hard automation were quite different from today's problems. With manufacturing production expanding, the human resource function was concerned with recruiting and retaining employees of all types at all levels. Now the human resource function is involved in trimming the work force while advancing company goals of improved efficiency and flexibility.

For many companies, introducing computer-based technology has been a chief means of pursuing improved productivity and, hence, profitability. In this process it is important for management to establish programs designed to ease the effects of technological change on employees. All companies would prefer to innovate without laying off any employees, and to that end, many try to introduce new technology during the upward phase of the business cycle. Only one company, however, reported that it had actually delayed introduction of new technology until surplus employees could be absorbed.

One of our major hypotheses was that the new technology would not have devastating effects on companies' work forces, and it has been substantiated. Although the nature of the technology is revolutionary, its implementation is being accomplished in an evolutionary manner. For a variety of reasons—technical, economic, and managerial—the new technology will continue to be introduced gradually, so companies will be afforded the time in which to plan to avoid large scale employee displacement. The best way of maintaining employment levels is to have sales, and hence production, grow as rapidly as the increase in productivity induced by the new technology, but this is not always possible.

Attrition

Even a declining need for employees, however, need not lead to employee dismissals if astute human resource management permits normal attrition to trim the work force before the change becomes effective. Effective utilization of attrition is the most helpful way of minimizing separation of employees. In addition, most multiplant companies have some flexibility in assignment of production and can shift work to plants with excess employees. Preventing layoffs resulting from change is often feasible because new technology tends to be introduced first in growth sectors of the business.

Some nonunion companies have full employment or employment stabilization policies whereby employees are never laid off. One of the companies with such a policy believes that it is beneficial to the company, as well as the employees. Since they are not fearful of losing their jobs, employees tend to be more loyal and even more productive.

To effectuate a no-layoff policy, companies establish buffers—temporary employees and contracting out—so that if new technology does reduce labor requirements, the buffer, not the regular full-time work force, absorbs it.[1] Such practices have been effective in adjusting work force size to cyclical shifts in demand for a company's products. In recent years, however, full employment companies have encountered serious difficulties as structural and technological changes have become severe. Some have been forced into crash programs to induce employees to leave voluntarily and even into laying off some workers when voluntary quits have not sufficiently reduced the work force.

Even being able to maintain a company's full employment policy does not mean that no workers are laid off elsewhere. For example, it was reported that when IBM cut back its purchases of disk drives from Tandon Corp. in 1985, this led to layoffs at Tandon.[2] IBM, however, by increasing its own disk drive production, was furthering its policy of not laying off employees.

Some people argue that such a use of contracting out of production merely shifts the burden of unemployment to the supplier, and thus there is no net advantage to society of a company's employment stabilization policy. Companies following no-layoff policies are aware of this, and, to prevent undue impact on their suppliers' work forces, some limit the amount purchased from each supplier; thus, if they cut back on contracting out, no one supplier is heavily affected.

We found only one company guaranteeing jobs in writing. The guarantee was in the collective bargaining agreement and specified that it applied only to those on payroll as of that date and only for the duration of the agreement. With normal turnover, the company's commitment is continually reduced over the three-year contract period. Subsequent to our fieldwork, another of the companies negotiated a job security arrangement that protects workers against job loss for any reason except a decline in business.

Careful planning is necesary if work force reductions are to be handled through attrition, but experience shows that, even with extensive change in technology, it is possible. The rate of labor turnover resulting from voluntary quits, retirements, and deaths, is fairly predictable, and this normal attrition can be used to effectuate any work force reduction that may be necessary as a result of new technology. If attrition is to be sufficient to avoid layoffs, however, companies must be careful not to inflate their work forces by new hiring prior to the introduction of new technology. Among the techniques that can be used in that period are more efficient utilization of the current work force, overtime work that can be eliminated as manpower requirements decline, the hiring of nonpermanent workers, and internal transfers and retraining to ensure that the work force is properly balanced in different operations.

Temporary Employees

Although the use of a flexible cadre of temporary employees in order to protect the jobs of regular employees is growing, it does not solve the employment problem from a societal point of view. As in the case of internal production in place of contracting out, someone still loses a job, no matter how the person is labeled. Mangum, Mayall, and Nelson have written, "As the practice of lifetime employment spreads, we can expect that the more workers who are guaranteed job security, the greater the number who will have to play the peripheral role to provide necessary human buffer."[3]

Companies follow two approaches to the use of temporary employees: hiring them directly and placing them on payroll or contracting with a temporary help service firm. Some companies that have directly hired temporary workers, however, have employed these workers for long periods of time and then discovered that they are as resentful of dismissal as regular employees would be. This approach also creates two different classes of employees within a company, one with virtual job security and the other with none.

The concept of the dual labor market arose in recent years as an explanation of the employment problems of minority groups.[4] According to the dual labor market hypothesis, the labor market is composed of a core, which provides stable jobs with adequate pay and fringe benefits and a career ladder, surrounded by a periphery of less stable activities with lower wages and intermittent work. Large companies, such as those in our study, are considered to be the major employers in the core and smaller firms in more competitive industries to comprise the periphery. The growth of competition in large-scale manufacturing during the past decade, however, has undercut the once-vaunted market power of the major companies[5] and, thus, their ability to maintain employment and work standards. With the increased use of temporary employees, some of these companies may be creating internal dual labor markets, with a core composed of regular employees with a measure of job security and a periphery of temporaries subject to the vagaries of economic movements.[6] The latter also would bear the brunt of the displacement caused by technological change.

All the companies with employment stabilization policies recognize the danger of creating a dual internal labor market. They try to avoid its development by strictly limiting the number and percentage of temporary employees. They also try to make sure that those hired for such positions truly want only temporary jobs. In the last few years, however, with high unemployment in many of the labor markets in which manufacturing operations are located, workers who want permanent jobs have settled for temporary ones.

The use of temporary employees for short-term needs is very sensible, especially during transition periods to new technology when both the old and new processes must be operated simultaneously. A plant that was introducing a flexible manufacturing system in one of its departments needed to train its regular work force for the new process, which was undergoing debugging. It also needed a large group of workers to operate the old process and to aid in the debugging. The plant used the services of a temporary hiring service, which provided it with 455 people at the peak of the transition. As phases of the training and debugging process were completed, the number needed gradually declined with the use of temporaries to be phased out completely, unless some new temporary need arose.

The strategy proved to be a success in that it enabled the plant to accomplish its goal of moving toward the new technology without manpower shortages and without first hiring and then having to lay off hundreds of employees, thereby damaging employee morale. The plant's human resource department, moreover, could not have made such a massive recruitment effort in that short a time. The temporary agency did all the screening, training, and paperwork. The only drawback to using the agency was that the plant was precluded from hiring any of the temporaries as full-time regular employees, which it would have liked to have done in many instances.

Early Retirement

The accomplishment of staff reductions through attrition can be speeded up through the use of various techniques, particularly by making early retirement financially attractive to older workers. Most of the study companies that have had to cut back their work forces, whether for economic or technological change reasons, did use early retirement.

One company that has offered special early retirement in order to reduce its work force does so only when it can find no other alternative because of the costliness of such programs. Early retirement not only has a high financial cost, but since a company cannot discriminate among employees meeting the requirements, it may lose people it considers essential. When early retirement was offered across the board in one company, the electrical engineer who had designed one plant's CIM system opted for it because of its generous features. From a societal point of view, large-scale early retirement may not be desirable. It wastes valuable human resources that could be contributing to national output, and it raises the costs of the private pension system. In some cases, moreover, its initial attraction to employees may fade during retirement, either because of boredom or a discovery that even the larger pension does not provide an acceptable income as the price level rises. Thus many early retirees do return to the labor market, usually in search of part-time work. Nevertheless, when a sufficient number of jobs is not available, there must be some way of rationing them.

Thus despite the drawbacks to special early retirement, companies have made heavy use of it, considering retiring older workers on a pension more equitable than laying off younger ones with greater financial needs and family obligations. Younger workers, the hope for the future, are often more amenable to retraining and thus work more effectively with the new technology. There is a danger with layoffs, moreover, in that a plant may not get back the workers it wants when they are recalled; given their skills, they may have been able to find other jobs. When layoffs are large, the gradual process of recall will not bring back many of the younger workers, who are considered more adaptable to new technology, because too many high-seniority people are ahead of them. By the time the young ones are reached, many of them will no longer be interested in returning.

Special early retirement programs have been very effective in reducing surplus manpower because they have been extremely generous. According to a study of companies offering early retirement incentives in 1984, the "most frequently offered was some form of monthly pension supplement or bridging payment, followed by actuarially unreduced pensions, one-time cash payments, salary continuation at a reduced level, and added service credit for faster vesting."[7] All these variants were used among the companies, and the liberality of the early retirement offers made it advantageous for older workers to accept them. At one plant that underwent heavy reductions in force, early retirement was the major means of accomplishing that reduction. Workers could retire as young as age 55 and receive 72 percent of the pension that they would have been entitled to at age 60, the normal age of retirement at that plant. As a result, 1,900 of the 3,200 employee reduction in force over a six-year period were people who retired on pensions.

Of the remaining 1,300 employees, most of whom were laid off, many moved away from the area, which was in general economic decline because of the depression in agriculture. Some were able to find other jobs locally, but a large number dropped out of the labor force entirely. Seventy percent of the affected work force was female and included many second earners. All labor market studies indicate that women have a tendency to leave the labor force when jobs become scarce.

Intraplant Transfers

Affecting transfers in order to prevent loss of employment is another principal element of human resources planning. The elimination of specific jobs by new technology requires the transfer of employees to others if they are to retain their attachment to the company work force. The absence of unionization obviously gives management great flexibility to move people about, but organized plants also can use transfers to avoid layoffs. Even when seniority rules are roadblocks to transferring displaced employees, joint labor-management solutions usually can be fashioned.

Company efforts to avoid technology-related layoffs can run into problems even when sufficient jobs exist because of mismatches between job requirements and worker skills. This problem is most acute when job classifications are narrow; a worker may be adept at performing a specific job, but when new technology eliminates that job, the person may be incapable of doing another one. Companies that have moved to broader job classifications and toward job rotation for reasons of both greater operating flexibility and improved employee motivation and job satisfaction have discovered these to offer an extra bonus. The employee who regularly does more than one specific task is less threatened that his or her job will be eliminated by change because he or she can more easily move into another.

The philosophy of the employee relations function, however, is of paramount importance in fashioning adjustments. At a plant where the employee relations stance traditionally has been reactive, not proactive, management did little to cushion the impact of change on employees; thirty-four workers were laid off following the introduction of automated casting in the foundry. Some of the laid-off workers had twenty-five years of service, while others in the foundry who kept their jobs had less than two. This occurred because management adhered to the collective bargaining agreement that specified departmental seniority. When it was suggested that some more equitable arrangement might have been worked out with the local, management's response was, "But the union didn't ask for it."

For most transfers caused by new technology, the worker is moved from one job to another within the same department. In some cases, the entire department may be affected by new processes, so the employees must be transferred elsewhere in the plant. We encountered numerous intraplant transfers that moved workers from one type of operation to a decidedly different one.

In transferring workers displaced by new technology, management seeks to provide them not only with alternative jobs but also with comparably compensated jobs. Retraining is provided so that they may qualify for similarly rated positions. Comparably paying jobs, however, are not always available, and this is particularly true of higher rated ones, in which few workers quit. A common technique, therefore, has been to give displaced workers transferring to other jobs rate protection ("red circle rates") for a period of time extended beyond that normally allowed.

Although red circle rates solve one set of problems, they can create others. While everyone in a plant understands the reasons for rate protection and is sympathetic to those who have been displaced, resentment does arise when workers doing the same job are compensated differently. Giving a large number of workers rate protection, moreover, tends to undermine a plant's wage structure. According to the experience of one of the companies that extends rate protection to workers displaced by technology, it takes about three years of normal attrition to work out the red circle rates and put a plant's wage structure back in line with its job evaluation system.

Interplant Transfers

In a few cases in which reduced labor requirements at a plant provided no opportunities for intraplant transfers, the workers were transferred to other company facilities. Interplant transfers, however, were far from usual. They were common mainly when a company had a number of plants in a particular labor market area, and workers could be transferred from one to another without the need to relocate.

Sometimes fortuitous events make interplant transfers possible. One company faced a sharp cutback in manpower requirements, partially due to new technology, at a plant in one of its divisions. At the same time, another division, which was experiencing product demand growth, sought company investment funds for expansion of one of its plants. Because the plants of the two divisions were within an acceptable commuting distance, corporate headquarters, under the prodding of the human resource function, made release of the funds sought by the expanding division contingent on its acceptance of the workers displaced at the plant of the declining division, and no employees lost jobs.

Interplant transfers are much more common for technical and managerial personnel than for blue-collar employees. Most companies are not willing to transfer production workers, preferring to recruit their work forces from local labor markets. One company that does not transfer workers at company expense to other locations does give preference to workers laid off at one plant for hiring at another. Workers hired at other plants retain their seniority for purposes of pension eligibility and other benefits but not for layoff and recall.

Interplant transfer is virtually impossible when different unions represent the workers at a company's various plants. In one case, however, a number of international unions representing the workers at different plants of a company did agree to a preferential hiring program for displaced workers.

A much more formidable barrier to interplant transfers, even when a company has a policy fostering them, is the reluctance of blue-collar workers to relocate. There is a large body of evidence on the lack of worker mobility (for example, because of home ownership, children in school, and friends and relatives in the community). In an era of escalating costs of housing and mortgages, home ownership became an extremely significant deterrent to willingness to accept interplant transfer. With the development of the dual-career family, the reluctance to accept transfers has spread into the professional and managerial ranks.

One company that follows a no-layoff policy is heavily dependent on interplant transfers to effectuate that policy. It does suffer from an available jobs–available skills mismatch and therefore was deeply disturbed by the reluctance of blue-collar workers to accept relocation. This reluctance was acute among those holding the lower-level jobs that are declining most rapidly at some of its plants as a result of advanced technology. So far the company has been able to maintain its policy of no layoffs despite new technology by transferring additional work into plants with surplus employees, but the company does not see this as a long-run solution to the problem, and it may have to require workers to relocate to retain jobs.

Another company's experience confounded all the accepted wisdom with respect to the relocation of production workers. Although the national collective bargaining agreement between the company and the union stated that a worker could move if his or her work is moved, decades of experience had shown that few workers are willing to relocate. In this instance, the production of a particular product was transferred from an old multiproduct plant in a large midwestern city to a new plant in a small community about 250 miles away in another state. In view of the general decline of industry in the old industrial city, management thought that a larger percentage than usual, perhaps as many as 400 of the 1,000 affected workers, would transfer, and the company began to recruit and train the rest of the work force at the new location. Then the 1980 recession set in, and the workers realized that there were virtually no other local jobs at comparable rates of pay for them, and so almost all 1,000 accepted relocation. Only the skilled tradesmen, for whom there were other job opportunities in the city, elected not to transfer.

The move was a rather traumatic experience, involving a change in culture from a large city to a small town. In many families, the workers' spouses and children did not want to relocate. Many of the transferees could not sell their houses in their original location, and the $1,246 relocation allowance provided by the company did not cover all their moving expenses. They moved, nonetheless, to keep their high-paying jobs.

The workers' acceptance of relocation caused community relations problems for the company at the new location. Since the skilled tradesmen did not transfer, it was able to hire ninety local people for those jobs, plus eighty salaried white-collar employees. The community, however, was extremely upset, having expected about 800 job openings.

The company started the process of moving people late in 1980 and continued it through the spring of 1981. The plant began operating in June 1981. Since the transferees were employees with fairly long service (average seniority was twelve years), four years later some were retiring, opening up job opportunities for people in the local labor market. Of more importance to the community, in October 1984, the plant added a second shift, and the national union agreed to the hiring of local people for most of the jobs. Thus 250 people from the community were hired, and the rest of the shift came from transferees from other company plants that had surplus workers.

Employee Reassignment

Elaborate programs for reassigning displaced employees exist among the companies. A computer manufacturer, for example, has established an employee placement center. All operating divisions needing workers submit their requirements to the center, which tries to fill the openings with displaced employees. The divisions cannot hire outside people for those jobs unless the center agrees, which it does only when it is unable to supply the requisite skills. The center engages in skill assessment. Since such analysis is labor-intensive work done by highly paid job analysts, the company is attempting to develop computer-based assessment techniques in a joint study by company industrial relations, engineering, and line management.

Benefits for Displaced Workers

In situations in which employees do lose their jobs, companies have not simply cast the workers aside but most often provide benefits of various types: severance pay, supplementary unemployment benefits, income continuance, job placement aid, and education and retraining assistance.

Severance pay is usually available to employees who are permanently laid off. The amount to which an individual is entitled may be based on a combination of age and service or on service only. A typical severance benefit is one week of pay for each year of service, paid either in a lump sum or monthly.

A number of companies provide supplementary unemployment benefits to laid-off workers. These may be available for as long as 104 weeks. In combination with state unemployment benefits, they provide laid-off employees with as much as 95 percent of normal take-home pay. Such benefits, sometimes called income extension aid, are more typical where a plant is covered under a national collective bargaining agreement.

Income guarantees also exist. In one company, workers with ten or more years' seniority are protected even after supplementary benefits run out. They can receive between 50 and 75 percent of take-home pay, depending on seniority, until age 62. The guarantee ends when another job is available to the covered worker.

Some companies that do not have an adequate number of jobs to which to transfer displaced employees have engaged in outplacement activities, contacting other potential employers and conducting job fairs. A few companies have trained displaced employees in new skills that would be used by other potential employers. Two companies are experimenting with business promotion centers through which they try to promote new small businesses and have them hire displaced employees. The company that has been doing this the longest offers training services to these businesses. Despite initial hopes, so far these centers have not been successful in generating job opportunities for blue-collar production workers.

8
The Nature of Jobs and the Organization of Work

Computer technology is having a profound effect on the nature of jobs and the ways in which work is organized. The scope of jobs is expanding. Workers are being trained to be more versatile and are being afforded greater responsibility and control over their work. The work environment also is undergoing change, becoming safer and cleaner.

The Changing Nature of Jobs

The first industrial revolution was characterized by the advent of power-driven machinery in a factory setting. While some division of labor did occur, it was limited by the fact that markets for most products also were quite limited. Workers' skills were fairly general, and they could operate a variety of new machine tools.

Mass Production and Scientific Management

The introduction of mass production in the late nineteenth and early twentieth centuries had a significant impact on management and on the organization of work. It was in this period that the concept of management developed. Previously most businesses had been small scale and owner operated. The few large factories, such as that of the Singer Sewing Machine Company in Elizabethport, New Jersey, were organized on the basis of independent contractors, themselves skilled workers, running the various operations within the plant. The Singer Elizabethport plant, which opened in 1873, did not abolish the inside contracting system until 1883.[1] The replacement of contractors with paid foremen was designed to increase management control over production and costs. Centralized management and control, however, evolved gradually and haphazardly, depending on the whims and judgments of individuals in charge.

It was in this era that Frederick W. Taylor and the scientific management movement had their impact. At this time, machine tools were set up and operated by skilled machinists acting on their own. In order to increase management control of the production process and operate with greater efficiency, Taylor advocated gathering the knowledge stored in the workers' heads. Rules-of-thumb ways of work then could be replaced with "scientifically" determined procedures.

With the introduction of mass production, Taylor's ideas precisely fit industry's needs. Following Adam Smith's dictum that the division of labor is limited by the extent of the market, as mass production expanded, management, in order to increase efficiency, broke jobs down into their constituent elements, creating the need for a mass of unskilled and semiskilled workers. The automobile assembly line came to epitomize the new way of organizing work.

Under the influence of Taylor's advocacy of the separation of planning from doing, production jobs were further restricted and all intellectual content removed from them. The people on the shop floor no longer did their own setup work; this became a function of newly emerging industrial engineering departments. In addition to specialization and further division of labor, the time and motion study of scientific management prescribed how the simplified job was to be done and how long it should take.

Mass production, management control, and work simplification increased productivity significantly and thereby facilitated an enormous rise in living standards in the industrialized countries. They also resulted in many production jobs becoming repetitive and boring. Thus there was a trade-off: much higher living standards for simplified jobs. Work became instrumental, no longer affording satisfaction except as a means to earn money to enjoy life outside the work environment. Because many jobs were arduous and uninteresting, moreover, management had to coerce workers to perform diligently. Problems of tardiness and absenteeism abounded.

Influence of New Technology

The nature of jobs and their design and organization are changing in response to computer-based technologies. Under the older system of mass production, the machinery was special purpose; it was devoted to performing a single function. Special-purpose machinery, in turn, begot special-purpose jobs.[2] Given the ability to reprogram machine tools in order to perform different tasks, the advent of computer-based technology is, in effect, a return to general-purpose machinery. As a result, jobs must become more general and shop floor workers more broadly skilled.

In the traditional system of work organization, jobs are arranged in a hierarchy of distinct, often multiple, classifications, each assigned a separate wage rate.[3] This system no longer fits the needs. With an emphasis on flexibility in manufacturing, there has to be greater flexibility in the utilization of the work force. Rigid demarcations must give way to multiskilled jobs, and compensation systems must be revised to reward workers for broadening their knowledge bases. Hourly employees need to gain greater control over their work and to be given more authority.

Motivational and reward systems also are in flux. As machine productivity becomes divorced from the actions of individual operators, traditional incentive systems, based on the individual's output, go by the boards. Companies are searching for ways to reward people's efforts, which remain important to the efficiency of system operation but are no longer easily measurable. One company has been able to maintain its incentive plan under programmable automation by placing greater emphasis on factors other than output (for example, reduction of downtime).

Employee involvement and expansion of the scope of jobs are becoming increasingly important because highly automated plants have a growing amount of integration and coordination at lower levels, pushing decision making downward.[4] Information, formerly a monopoly of managers, may become available to workers on the shop floor, enabling them to act on their own. The discretionary parts of jobs increase, and employees must diagnose problems in order to prevent system interruptions. According to Hirschhorn, "The new cybernetic machines create new sources of error and failure with which only skilled workers, ready to learn and adapt to new production conditions, can contend."[5]

To date, only a few companies have expanded jobs to include operator control of processes. In discussion with managers, two reasons emerged, one technical and the other ideological. The technical explanation is that many data bases do not yet provide sufficient information to operators on the plant floor. In fact, the development of data bases often has paralleled the pyramidal organization structure with its stress of managerial perogatives. Sapor has bluntly stated, "Information is power, and access to it remains a clear badge of rank to managers."[6] Operators will not gain control if management is reluctant to allow them such control.[7] Some managements, however, have been more willing to share power with their employees, pointing to a movement toward a more versatile, higher skilled work force.

One high-tech company is following a definite strategy with respect to the changing nature of jobs and that is to allow employees to maximize their capabilities. People at lower levels now have more autonomy, and there is a development of more transferable skills. Companies must provide the necessary information, which computerization makes possible, so that the people on the floor can exercise autonomy. At the same time, many repetitive and boring jobs or those involving heavy labor, such as in grinding operations, are being eliminated through the use of automated machines. This company's goal is to create a hierarchy of jobs, with employee opportunity to move to higher-level ones as lower-level ones are eliminated.

A nonsynchronous line was introduced in an assembly operation in an appliance plant, with the employees gaining some control over their own work. This move was dictated by the company's new stress on quality; management did not want the assemblers to rush to keep up with the line, because this causes shoddy workmanship and many rejects. Each assembler now has three controls: one to stop the line at his or her station; a second to send completed work on to the next station; and a third to send an item to repair in case of a major defect. At some points, the assemblers can adjust the height of the line so that they can either sit or stand to do their tasks.

A new venture of one company is being used as a laboratory in which to try out new ideas. Traditional job classifications have been modified and production workers are being given a voice in decision making. Teamwork is the key to the new work organization. In an assembly operation, an individual can stop the line if he or she believes something is wrong. This is having a positive impact on morale and also yielding a better product. Another work organization innovation is the transfer of responsibility for setup from industrial engineering people to the hourly employees. Overall there has been a sharp increase in output per worker.

Deskilling and Upskilling

Not all types of jobs benefit from new technology in terms of skill. Because programming of NC machines is being done either by engineers or special programmers working in offices, machinists have been deskilled. One facility tried to temper this adverse impact on machinists by having them do all the setup work on the NC machines. We found, however, that the replacement of the NCs with CNC machines had the effect of making the machinist's job somewhat more meaningful. Under the NC, programming was done entirely off-line, reducing the machinist to a machine tender; with the CNCs, the machinist does some of the programming on-line, a decided improvement in the nature of the job.

Similarly some testers have been deskilled since all they do now is monitor a computer, where formerly they had to exercise judgment. This is an unfortunate consequence as far as job content is concerned but a decidedly beneficial one with respect to product quality. At a plant manufacturing aircraft instrumentation, computer testing has reduced defects by 70 percent, and the test technician now spends more time logging data than actually testing parts.

Other workers, particularly operators, have been upskilled through enlarged job duties, including problem solving and setup work. In many plants, the number of separate jobs is being reduced so that workers can perform a greater variety of tasks. For example, management and the union in one plant negotiated a marked reduction in job classifications. Where formerly there had been 125 different ones, including more than 20 for skilled tradesmen, there are now only 25 production worker classifications and 8 skilled ones.

One intriguing issue revolves around who does the programming of computer-controlled machines; our research revealed no uniformity among companies. Some assign the role exclusively to engineers or special programmers, others split the function, with special programmers doing off-line and production workers, on-line, programming, and still others have shop floor workers perform most of the programming.

Since American practice diverges from that of other countries, where production workers do much more of the programming, we searched for explanations of the difference. According to Thurow, it lies in the lesser capabilities of American workers: "Foreign numerically controlled machines can be 'unlocked' since the blue-collar workers can be taught to do the necessary programming, while American machine tools are 'locked' partly because blue-collar workers cannot easily be taught the necessary programming."[8] We found limited support for his contention, with only a few managements having concluded that their computer processes are too complicated for production workers. A much more cogent explanation lies in the labor relations area—a management desire to keep programming out of the bargaining unit in unionized situations. This desire is based on the fear that if the job is in the bargaining unit, it will be subject to stringent rules on demarcation and seniority bumping procedures, which could threaten flexibility of operations and result in extraordinary training costs and inefficient operations as untrained workers bump into positions involving programming.

Some companies have no organization-wide policy with respect to who does the programming. There are even inconsistencies within plants. In one of a company's plants, programming is done by manufacturing engineering, except for painting robots, which are programmed by former painters. In its other plants, operators program even the NC machines.

Since programming a robot is not difficult, many companies find that it makes sense to retrain production workers as programmers. This is particularly true in walk-through teaching of robots, but even off-line programming may be within the ability of the workers. Their knowledge of the operation, moreover, may make them better at the job. Similarly, many robot technicians are being trained in two-year colleges, but in this instance, too, companies are finding it more expedient to retrain present workers. General Motors, for example, has reached agreement with the United Auto Workers that robot technicians will come from the ranks of skilled trades.

One company has a novel approach to the programming issue. Programming is done not by hourly employees but by a separate programming group. All the people in that group, however, come from the hourly ranks. But even this approach has not become a hard and fast rule, for at one of its plants, operators have been trained to operate computer consoles and over time will be given programming responsibilities.

One heavily unionized company has a formal understanding that any work done within the bargaining unit remains there despite technological change. Thus bargaining unit people do the on-line programming of machines. As the jobs of welders and spray painters are robotized, these workers do the programming of the robots, and electricians are responsible for their maintenance. Electricians are being converted into electronic technicians.

Broadening Jobs

A major reason for broadening production workers' jobs is that computer technology is complex and thus subject to breakdown. In just about every plant visited, some part of the system was out of commission while we were there. Where shop floor workers have been provided with some understanding of the operation, they can make adjustments themselves when breakdowns occur, so production is not halted for long periods until someone from maintenance can look at the equipment. In these plants, production workers are trained to diagnose possible malfunctions and engage in preventive maintenance. In fact, some plants are moving toward a new type of job: an operator-maintenance category.

The problem of maintenance of sophisticated computerized equipment keeps arising. Many of the plants therefore have enlarged production worker jobs to include preventive maintenance, but this is not always possible. In some plants, it has been blocked by the fact that production and maintenance are two separate units and the unions are loathe to agree to the mixing of their duties. Inspectors, too, often are a separate seniority group, so the operators are not permitted to do any inspection. Plant managements are conferring with the unions in attempts to reduce the number of separate seniority units so that operator jobs can be expanded to include preventive maintenance.

The need for preventive maintenance was identified at one plant through quality circles. Its management therefore trained the operators in maintenance duties and in programming of computerized machines. From every point of view, including that of operator morale, the training has been successful. It shows in cleaner work areas, for example. As a result of preventive maintenance, the plant achieved a $60,000 savings in maintenance costs in one year. Most important, it has been a boon to efficient operation, since under automation, if one process goes down, the whole system ceases working.

At a flexible manufacturing center under development in another plant, management had to prepare new job descriptions. In the process, it discovered that the operators had to be trained to assume greater responsibility, including preventive maintenance. The training was successful, but management learned that it is better to train by stages rather than in leaps, which might have overwhelmed the workers.

In a unionized appliance plant, all thirty workers in an automated plastic molding operation were divided into autonomous work teams. Differences in job titles, duties, and pay were eliminated, and one new higher grade was established. Everyone was trained to operate the system and to make minor repairs to keep it functioning. The work teams establish their own schedules of who is responsible for what duty each day, from sweeping the floor to monitoring the system. This organization ensures less downtime, and it also eliminates problems stemming from absenteeism because everyone can perform the most important tasks.

One problem caused by giving operators some maintenance authority is jurisdictional disputes with maintenance, which resents production workers' making adjustments to machinery. Maintenance workers fear a loss of status and job opportunities. The problem is particularly acute, and can lead to many grievances, when production and maintenance workers are represented by different unions. Even so, managements have concluded that the advantages outweigh the labor relations difficulties.

Broadening job classifications is extremely important to cost reduction. The production process does not always operate in a smooth, continuous flow, and thus there are periods in which work may not be available for all job classifications. The narrower are the classifications, the more difficult it is to reassign idled workers to other tasks, and they stand around doing nothing but drawing pay. With broader classifications, it is much more likely that other work is available for the employees. This greater flexibility in the utilization of the work force is one of the most significant advantages of nonunion plants.

One way to broaden classifications without incurring union opposition is to include setup work in the job. The setup and operation classification is growing rapidly at a plant manufacturing electronic control devices. In management's view, since the worker has set the job up, he or she has a feeling of ownership, in contrast to the former attitude, "I only run the machine." The job has expanded because the operator can make adjustments; if the worker cannot diagnose the problem, he or she calls for help from maintenance. The operator now spends more time monitoring and is in charge of five machines, with the emphasis placed on quality. Operators are subject to less boredom than formerly since they perform a number of different tasks, and employees are satisfied with the variety. With respect to qualifications for new jobs, this plant's selection criteria include not only ability but also willingness to be retrained.

Another high-tech company has a similar approach. Its skill mix is changing to fewer low-skill jobs and more high-skill ones. Its policy is to hire a person for the next level, not the job that the individual will be doing at the beginning. The local personnel director and the engineers in each plant determine its skill needs. In this case, too, the rising skill levels are evidenced in the greater maintenance abilities of the operators.

Another electronics producer found that as a result of new technology, jobs throughout the plant have tended to become more complex and the workers, as a result, more skilled. In order to introduce greater variety, management rotates workers from station to station rather than have them perform one task day after day. The major technological change introduced in this plant, however, was the conversion of its warehouse to an ASRS, which dramatically changed the nature of jobs. Formerly it had been primarily physical labor, such as lifting, placing, and climbing ladders, but since the robots now do those tasks, there is little physical effort involved. Instead the workers are intimately involved with computers, inputting the data needed. Former unskilled laborers are now workers with skills—skills that are transferable in the labor market as more companies move toward ASRS.

The Work Environment

One incontrovertible conclusion with respect to new computer-based technology is that it is creating a safer work environment. The major uses of robots have been in materials handling, welding, spray painting, and machine loading, jobs that are strenuous and/or dangerous to the health and safety of workers. Robots are now performing much of the arduous physical labor.

Although safety considerations have not been a major motivation for the introduction of the new technology, safety has been a contributing and, in a few instances the primary, reason. This was the case at a plant utilizing nuclear materials where robots were installed in order to minimize workers' exposure to radiation.

At another plant, safety was greatly increased by the automation of a line for gold plating. Formerly all the employees in the operation had been exposed to sulfuric acid fumes and subject to burns since they physically dipped bags of items to be gold plated into the solution and then transferred the bags by hand to the next solution. The hand system still is being used for short runs, and the contrast in terms of safety between that and the automated line is extreme. For most workers in the unit, therefore, the jobs are now easier and safer.

The safety advantages of new technology were well illustrated by a dramatic incident at one plant in which giant hydraulic presses were utilized in the production process. Robots had replaced workers in feeding items into and removing them from the presses. One day a robot was mangled due to a malfunction in the timing of the press. Under the old system, a human being would have been killed.

At another plant, safety was significantly improved by a change in the composition of the product, as well as the use of new technology. The technology was the use of robots in the dangerous and strenuous work. The product change was a substitution of molded plastic for steel in the product, which eliminated the cuts and gashes formerly suffered by workers. As a result, the accident rate in the plant declined 31 percent—from 8.7 percent (OSHA reportable) before the change to a 6.0 percent after.

The introduction of ASRSs also has meant a decline in physical work and accidents associated with it. In one plant, there has been a virtual elimination of injuries in the warehouse; it has declined from twenty active cases at any time to two to three. Workers do much less lifting of heavy packages and no longer have to climb ladders to put parts into or remove them from the bins. ASRS also has permitted storing in more manageable units; where a package used to weigh seventy-five pounds, it is now no more than forty-five pounds, so any lifting that a worker must engage in is easier than before.

Another plant was in the process of automating an operation for the sole purpose of eliminating a health hazard. The operation involved the intricate assembly of very small pieces, and many of the workers were contracting carpal tunnel syndrome of the wrist as a result.

Safety can be a problem in a new plant, even an automated one, because of unfamiliarity with the equipment. One plant that opened in 1976 has an average 12 percent OSHA reportable accident rate over its history. Since this included the startup years, when experience was first being gained, it has declined substantially over the years. By 1984, the rate was down to 8 percent, which management conceded was still poor. The high accident rate was ascribed to the fact that the work force has been engaged in a good deal of overtime work, with accompanying fatigue.

Accident rates vary by industry; a plant utilizing heavy presses or engaged in metal casting operations will be susceptible to more injuries than one assembling small electronic products. The important statistic, therefore, is not the accident rate but its reduction following the introduction of new technology. A plant manufacturing aircraft electronics and instrumentation had a very low OSHA incidence rate of 1.4 percent in 1979 before it brought in computer-based automation. Even that low rate dropped by 43 percent, to 0.8 by 1985, as a result of the new technology.

Robots and other forms of programmable automation have made a significant contribution to overall plant safety, but they also can cause accidents if not properly controlled. There have been reports in the press of workers injured and even killed by computer-operated equipment (for example, crushed by a robot). A coalition of eight unions has been pressing for an effective lockout standard for robots and all other computer-operated equipment. Such a standard would require the de-energization of industrial robots and other types of computer-operated equipment during maintenance and would call for set procedures to mechanically prevent inadvertent activation.[9]

The problem is complex. Employee safety is paramount, yet shutting off all power to ensure such safety could lead to loss of computer memory. One plant studied had devised a system whereby anyone coming within a certain radius of a robot automatically triggered its shutdown. The system was completely effective in preventing workers from being injured by robots, but the robots were frequently being needlessly shut down when a worker from another department walked too close to the robot or visitors on plant tours leaned too far over the robot area boundary line.

Computer-based technologies also tend to make for cleaner factories and workstations. Machine operators always get grease and oil on themselves, but this ceases when their jobs are converted to monitoring consoles. Only when there is a malfunction in the automated equipment must the worker even dirty his or her hands, and possibly not even then, because he or she may be able to correct the situation by pressing a button.

In one case, a decidedly improved working environment arose less from the technology than from a management desire to elicit worker cooperation in successfully implementing the technology. To this end, even before the introduction of the new technology, management established a new cafeteria within the plant. The cafeteria is not only clean and attractive but saves the workers from having to walk to another building for something to eat. Since the lunch period is only thirty minutes, this was highly appreciated by the work force. This plant was particularly clean, with no papers lying about on the floor, a sharp contrast to many other plants. Obviously management's stress on attractive surroundings has led the work force to respond by not littering the factory and keeping their own workstations neat.

Problem Areas

One area of controversy concerns computer monitoring of work performance. In assembly operations, for example, every piece of the final product can be identified in terms of who inserted it and when. Workers therefore may feel that they are subject to greater supervision, and some observers claim that this is a negative impact of the new technology on work. Others do not believe that workers resent computer monitoring, for they too want to know whether they are doing their work properly.

We found no evidence of worker reaction, positive or negative, to computer monitoring, and in only one plant did it become an issue. Even in this instance, the issue was not monitoring but the availability of the information. The union insisted that the workers and their stewards, as well as management, should have access to the data. In compliance with the union's wishes, consoles displaying work performance data were placed on the shop floor, as well as in the control room. Thus workers can supervise their own performance without awaiting negative feedback from their foremen, and the union has the same information as management in case of controversy concerning any individual's performance.

New technology, however, has had a negative impact on one aspect of the work context in some cases: social isolation in the factory because human-manned work stations become physically farther apart. Social isolation occurred in one operation as a result of automating the conveyor line that brought work to assemblers. Formerly, two tables, with one assembler at each, were placed next to each other. The automated line, however, separated the two physically, and the noise prevented communication between them.

When employees complained, management reversed its policy of banning radios and tapedecks from the work area. Now assemblers can wear headphones and listen to radios and tapes. Although the workers still do not have the opportunity for social interaction except during breaks, they have some connection with human voices or music. Management also permits the assemblers to take their allotted time for breaks whenever they wish because the conveyor moves continually and the person at the other side may pick up the piece to be worked on instead.

An official of a union representing workers at another plant saw employee involvement programs as one means of dealing with social isolation. According to him, quality team meetings are a substitute for the former interaction of employees while working.

Most workers are capable of working within a team approach, but some are not. In one plant, the six employees operating a computerized casting machine initially agreed to the team concept of work with job rotation but later rejected it despite a $1 per hour premium because one worker was afraid of doing one of the operations; work group solidarity led to the whole plan's being scrapped.

A serious impediment to expansion of job content may be the absence of worker motivation to increase knowledge and versatility. Some workers are not concerned with decision making and want nothing more from their jobs than to put in their time doing what they are told to do. In a discussion, a setup worker in one plant volunteered that people will learn only as much as they are being paid for and will not stretch themselves. She also claimed that many operators are lazy and want everything done for them. In the vast majority of plants, however, most workers, although sometimes fearful of the additional responsibilities being thrust upon them, welcomed the opportunity to broaden their work and gain greater control over it.

9
Employee Involvement

Development of Employee Involvement

The most dramatic change in the organization of work with the introduction of computer-based technology is greater employee involvement in decision making about their work. The most common approach is to hold regular meetings of the work group and its supervisor to discuss production problems and to innovate solutions to them. Generically these meetings have come to be known as quality circles, but they vary greatly with each situation. In a few cases, employee involvement in decision making has gone well beyond regular meetings of the work group. We have found examples of the application of sociotechnical systems theory, with its stress on teamwork. The major features of this new way of organizing work are:

1. Worker autonomy in carrying out assignments.
2. Flexibility in job assignments, with each worker capable of and actually performing different tasks, with accompanying pay for knowledge.
3. Teamwork, with group interaction and commitment.

The Japanese are far ahead of the United States in the application of computer-based technologies, and they also have led American industry in the implementation of organizational reform. According to the Japanese, the two most important factors facilitating the installation and smooth acceptance of robots in Japanese manufacturing companies have been the widespread existence of small group activities in their plants and in-house training programs and job rotation.[1] The objectives of small group activities, which include quality circles and project teams, are to improve productivity, reduce costs, ensure quality, and prevent accidents. Groups that achieve success receive widespread recognition in Japan.

American industry has lagged far behind in innovations in human resource management. Some of the problems of General Motors, for example, have been attributed to its underestimation of improved performance that could be achieved through better management of human workers and less investment in programmable automation.[2] Reportedly GM was surprised by the greater productivity achieved by employees in its former Fremont, California, plant when it reopened as a joint venture with Toyota under Japanese management.

American industry, however, is beginning to recognize the need to change its attitudes toward its workers. One of the most unanticipated findings of our study has been the extent to which American management is being converted, albeit belatedly and slowly, to a belief in employee involvement. Computer-based technologies can increase productivity, product reliability, flexibility, and workplace safety, but they still need people to operate them. As a result, companies have discovered that people are equally important to the accomplishment of organizational objectives. A British study group from the electrical machinery industry that visited North America reported that the introduction of programmable automation by itself can lead to significant productivity gains, but that without new organizational approaches, at least 40 percent of the realizable benefits are lost.[3] At one plant visited, a manager who is an expert in and consultant to the federal government on programmable automation advanced the idea that changing employee attitudes may be more important than technology in improving productivity and the way to change attitudes is through work design innovation.

The opportunity presented by new technology is that its introduction can be combined with a recognition of the importance of the human contribution. Line managers and even engineers, as well as employee relations specialists, have stressed this and have called attention to the fact that the workers on the plant floor are well educated and have tremendous potential for growth. They find beneficial regular meetings with employees to report on progress and any difficulties encountered with new technology. Employee involvement has been particularly crucial in efforts to improve product quality.

Those who have tried employee involvement are pleased with the results to date. Involvement in the planning and implementation of new processes has helped employees to become receptive to them and to the changes required of themselves. There is an upsurge in employee suggestions for greater efficiency; in one facility, 68 percent of the hourly employees turned in ideas that have saved the company $300 or more each. (Before the employee involvement program, under the old suggestion system, only 6 percent had offered such ideas.)

There is no magic formula for employee involvement. No company has found the perfect vehicle; they are experimenting with quality circles, autonomous production teams, and the like. One company started its program with the quality of work life (QWL) approach. (QWL is a form of employee involvement in which unionized workers, as members of small groups, cooperate with management outside formal collective bargaining procedures to improve the quality of the work life experience while enhancing productive efficiency.) QWL was even written into its collective bargaining contract, but over the years this form has been evolving toward self-managing work groups. Both management and labor are considering the development of problem-solving teams and augmenting involvement with some form of gains-sharing arrangement.

The degree of employee involvement on the shop floor depends largely on the unit manager. If he or she is enthusiastic about the process, subordinates will want to participate. If the manager only goes through the motions, the workers will respond accordingly. Union opposition also can undermine efforts to achieve a more participatory approach.

In some cases, employee involvement has not depended on formal programs. One person who was involved in a successful program was dubious about quality circles and the like. In his view, good management means continuous employee involvement, so he sees no need for formal mechanisms, such as quality circles. His view may be utopian at this time, when companies are only beginning to involve employees in work-related decision-making, but as the process continues, he may turn out to be correct.

Union Attitudes toward Employee Involvement

Union attitudes toward employee involvement vary, covering the entire gamut from active advocacy to forbidding their members to participate in the programs. In all cases, the initiative for involvement came from management, and then the union responded, negatively, positively, or halfheartedly, but most often positively. The positive union response can be illustrated by the experience of one company.

Management's concern with employee involvement stemmed from its recognition that automation designed to improve product quality could do so only with employee cooperation. The QWL program was built on the long-standing record of labor-management cooperation between the company and the union local.

The company's case for employee involvement rests on the skill, intelligence, and education of its labor force and an industrial relations culture that is different from the typical adversarial one. Management offered three assumptions underlying the direction in which it is moving:

1. The belief that more could be done to motivate employees, in effect changing the ethos of the work force.
2. The knowledge that employees have a lot to offer.
3. The conviction that, in order to survive, since the company's share of the product market has dropped drastically as a result of domestic and foreign competition, it must get the employees involved in helping to solve production problems.

It is fortunate that the union representing the company's production employees is equally enthusiastic about employee involvement.

Today numerous approaches come under the umbrella of QWL, but its history goes back to the mid-1970s when research began. As early as 1977, this company's labor-management agreement stated the intention of introducing employee involvement. Although the union represented workers in industries far removed from those represented by the United Auto Workers (UAW), it was highly influenced by the UAW's ideas, especially as formulated by its vice-president, Donald Ephlin. The next step was to bring in a consultant to formulate the program but the consultant so irritated the union however, that the program was almost scuttled. People more acceptable to the union took over, and employee involvement began. The design was formulated in 1979, and in 1980, it was formally negotiated with the union.

Employee involvement at this company has played an important role in its adjustment to new technology. In addition to examining issues directly related to their work, the teams examine each product market in which the company competes. Recognizing the need to be more competitive, they participate in such decisions as whether to make or buy components. The teams even have come up with suggestions for new technology.

An interesting development has been foremanless work groups. This form evolved from manpower reductions rather than from the nature of new technology, but the process technology did lend itself to the concept, and management did not replace redundant foremen. Management is even considering a general policy of having a supervisor only on call in case of emergencies. In some operations, hourly workers are setting production schedules, planning their work, and scheduling their own vacations. The company also is considering the group leader approach, although its experience with this in the past was unsatisfactory because once a worker was in such a position, he or she started acting as a supervisor—bossing fellow workers and not doing any work himself or herself.

The opposite end of the spectrum of union attitudes toward employee involvement is illustrated by the experience of an automobile plant. Although the national union is favorably disposed toward involvement, the local leadership is adamantly opposed, viewing it merely as a technique to co-opt the union. Therefore no formal program exists, although management does promote meetings by supervisors and their subordinates to discuss matters relating to work.

The problem has become more intractable because in a hotly contested union election, the winners' platform opposed involvement. Despite the more favorable attitude of the rank and file, management cannot persuade the union leadership that a QWL program would prevent many problems from arising. The local leadership has acceded a bit to the more pro-involvement attitudes of its members, however, by no longer forbidding them to participate in work group meetings, and many of them do so on a voluntary basis.

The company ascribes part of the problem of union leadership attitudes at this plant to the fact that it did not suffer layoffs in the 1981–1982 economic downturn. The greater was the impact of the recession, the more attitudes had changed, with those plants that had been shut down now enjoying the most cooperative relationships.

Management Attitudes toward Employee Involvement

Attitudes toward employee involvement among managers are as varied as those of union locals. As a result, involvement is not evenly distributed within companies, with some units being much further advanced than others and some still struggling to get their programs off the ground. Usually top management promulgates employee involvement as company policy but does not mandate that all units adopt it.

Middle managers in particular often are a major barrier to the implementation of employee involvement. Feeling threatened by it, they may sabotage it by withholding vital information or rejecting all suggestions offered by work groups. To overcome middle managers' resistance to employee involvement, a company must take steps to see that they too are involved in the program.

Middle management fears are not entirely groundless. The combination of a changing management philosophy—one of seeking to operate with a more organic than a mechanistic approach—and employee involvement, which is part of the organic style, is eliminating layers of middle management. Under the circumstances, top management can allay middle managers' fears only to the extent that it can assure them of continued employment.

Even where there is no resistance to employee involvement, the program can run out of steam, as happened at one of the plants in our study. The plant had been beset with a large number of operating problems, and when the work groups were organized in circles, they devoted their attention to solving them. Once the most obvious difficulties were overcome, the meetings of many of the work groups degenerated into bull sessions.

There also are serious philosophic differences within management concerning a greater role in decision making for hourly employees. The vice-president of personnel of one company asserted that headquarters does not encourage it. In his view, the way to get better performance is by announcing that without it the plant will be closed. He believes that employee involvement may start out well, but that is only a Hawthorne effect, and performance starts slipping again quickly. In fact, employee involvement can be detrimental, he believes, because it leads management to pay less attention to results. In this company, productivity is considered to be the line manager's responsibility, and decision making will go no further down than to first-line supervision.

This philosophy, however, did not permeate the entire company, and an involvement program was in operation at one of its plants. Top plant management took the position that, with automation, control of quality should be given to the operators; they have the instruments and should be trained to use them. Quality circles were operating in the plant. Management also is developing work cells with autonomy and giving workers more decision making with respect to quality and scheduling. The workers have responded favorably; they like the greater autonomy and job enrichment. Lower-level managers, however, resent their loss of power and have reacted strongly; higher management recognizes that it will take time to foster a new atmosphere.

Fostering greater worker autonomy and involvement is not always necessary. At a shipyard, the entire work force is composed of craftsmen, and a boss-worker atmosphere has never existed. Management is concerned with winning employee trust, not pushing people to produce more. There are no repetitive processes. Ninety-five percent of the supervisors come from the ranks and therefore are themselves craftsmen, who respect the abilities of the people assigned to their crews. On occasion, a new supervisor will start out acting bossy, and his crew will do exactly what he tells them to do. Inevitably he forgets to mention some detail, so they do not perform that necessary operation; he learns his lesson and henceforth relies on the good judgment and skills of his crew. Thus although there are no such mechanisms as quality circles, there is worker autonomy and involvement. In effect, the craftsmen are self-managing because of the nature of the work. In fact, without any formal program, the workers are involved in the planning and implementation of new technology; for example, there is feedback from the mechanics involved to the engineer designing a new process on his drawings, the machinery the engineer is proposing, and the like.

Technology and Involvement

I do not want to posit a strict doctrine of technological determinism, for other factors are at play in advancing new approaches to work organization. The severe competitive problems American industry faces also have challenged long-established authoritarian methods of management. The new technology, which requires greater cooperation among all members of the work force, helps to undermine authoritarianism.

Authoritarian control of the work force, however, was already breaking down. Directive supervision was a product of an earlier age when manufacturing was growing rapidly and absorbing large numbers of new industrial workers, many of them barely literate immigrants with peasant backgrounds. That era is long gone. A better-educated labor force, schooled to believe in democratic principles, has been increasingly reluctant to work under authoritarian control at routine jobs. The persistence of Taylorism consequently backfired in terms of its major goal: increased productivity of the manual worker. A system that put all decision making in the hands of supervisors destroyed worker motivation and denied employers the benefit of ideas that workers could have contributed to better production methods.

Management at one company admitted that by the 1960s, it had simplified jobs to the point that work had become so uninteresting that it had an impact on the quality of products; bored workers did not care. New technology is building some interest into jobs, and beyond that, job classifications are being merged into wider-scope jobs. There also had been an assumption by management that workers do not want responsibility and seek only to take orders from their foremen, but it was off the mark on this as well, for it has since discovered that workers are eager to acquire new skills and prefer less directive supervision.

A new venture of this company is being used as a laboratory in which to try out new ideas. Traditional job classifications have been modified, and production workers are being given more responsibility and participation in decision making. Also, management is more willing to examine workers' problems and attempt to deal with them. Teamwork is the key to the new work organization, and management is trying to instill the team concept throughout the plant. In an assembly operation, an individual can stop the line if he or she believes something is wrong, and this has a positive impact on morale. It is also yielding a higher-quality product. When the line stops, other workers do clean-up and similar chores, in contrast to earlier times when workers simply sat around and read newspapers during downtime. Another work organization innovation is set up by the hourly employees. Although the plant is not as automated as some of the company's others, it has doubled its output per worker.

Technology is not the sole factor in fostering new approaches to work organization but is a significant factor in making them possible. General Motors's new assembly plants to be opened in Kansas City, Kansas, and Doraville, Georgia, will eschew the traditional assembly line, with individual workers doing simple repetitive tasks. At the new plants, motorized, unmanned carriers called automated guided vehicles will carry a car through the process. The vehicles will stop at various locations, where groups of workers will perform logical blocks of work, such as installing the accessories on an engine. The carrier will leave a workstation only when released by the team. This approach would not have been possible without new technology. "We couldn't have done this a few years ago," said a GM official. "We need computers that can keep track of hundreds of carriers and decide on a minute-by-minute basis what station to assign them to, based on variations in the model mix."[4]

Contrasting Views

Not everyone agrees that programmable automation yields benefits to workers. Shaiken, for example, paints a dismal picture of computer-based technology's impact on work organization.[5] In his view, "The current shop floor organization intensifies work and reduces autonomy on the job."[6]

The differences between Shaiken's and our findings partly reflect the different cases we examined. He has concentrated on metalworking industries that make heavy use of robots and NC machines. There is a danger that workers could become robot sitters, but we found that this did not occur frequently. A welder who was now in charge of programming and operating a robot welder indicated great satisfaction with his new duties. Moreover, the industries we examined tend to concentrate on computerized control of production processes, and the experience therefore has been more favorable and has included job expansion and employee involvement.

Part of our differences, however, relate to philosophic outlooks. Shaiken and his associates claim that worker participation programs are part of an "ideology of competition" promoted by management to make workers believe that greater efficiency and job security are related. Employee involvement efforts thus "encourage workers to adopt a managerial perspective when production problems arise on the shop floor and to gain personal satisfaction from contributing ideas that promote efficiency." We do not quarrel with this statement; on the contrary, we believe it is necessary to have such worker attitudes, for without them, American manufacturing will not reestablish its competitiveness.

Sociotechnical Approaches

In a few cases, we found examples of the application of sociotechnical approaches to work organization. Sociotechnical theory can be traced to the work of the Tavistock Institute on job design and productivity in British coal mining.[7] The thesis was that an industrial organization is a structured sociotechnical system in which people and technology interact and are interdependent. At the same time, a number of American behavioral scientists were concentrating on motivation of workers through job enrichment, stressing the need for skill variety, task identity, task significance, autonomy, and feedback.[8] These theories led to the development of the idea of autonomous work groups, in which members share much of the decision making about the planning and execution of work.[9] The task is designed so that it is a whole process of work on which members can perform a variety of functions. An important element of such an organization of work is that there must be feedback to the group.

Volvo, in the interest of improving the quality of work life (a major Swedish goal), began experimenting with job rotation in the mid-1960s and finally replaced the assembly line characteristic of automobile production with self-managing work groups. Around the same time, a few U.S. companies began to experiment in new plants with such innovations. The new approach gave management greater flexibility in work force utilization, and it also seemed to be an important factor in keeping those plants nonunion. According to Verma and Kochan, "Workers today have acquired a taste for a cooperative, productive, and informal workplace" rather than one "characterized by conflict, legalistic, and impersonal work rules."[10]

GM's experience, however, shows that sociotechnical work organization need not be used as a union-avoidance device. Although GM used such approaches in its nonunion plants, it continued them after the UAW organized the plants.[11] The two parties agreed to utilize the sociotechnical system as part of the new Saturn compact car division. Our study also found examples of sociotechnical work organization in unionized plants.

The severe economic downturn of 1981–1982 made many more companies willing to examine the way they organize work. They are using the introduction of new technology also to experiment with job expansion and employee involvement, thus giving shop floor workers greater freedom to guide their own activities. Management's aim is not simply to make work more interesting but to increase efficiency thereby.

The most revolutionary approaches to the organization of work that we have come across are those in a synthetics plant, a cable plant, and a steel mill. The production workers' jobs have changed dramatically in all three operations.

The synthetics plant, which is a network of computer-operated and number-controlled systems, has only two production job grades: technician and production assistant. There are three types of technician: computer equipment technician, who repairs circuit boards, laser readers, power supply, and computer equipment; mechanical technician, who oversees hydraulic alignment, motor replacement, and transformer rotator alignment; and systems technician. The systems technician, who comes closest to the process operator in an older type of plant, manages the production flow, operates computers and peripheral equipment, analyzes problems and corrects short-term ones, records data, and furnishes assistance. There are no separate maintenance workers or foremen, since the technicians perform most of those functions.

All three plants use the team concept in work organization. The cable plant, which has been operating with a sociotechnical approach for a decade, divides the work force into autonomous work teams of about ten employees each (figure 9–1). A team meets at the beginning and end of each shift and is responsible for such direct work-related matters as production scheduling and monitoring and work assignment and such personnel matters as scheduling of hours, hiring and firing, discipline, and peer evaluation. There are no supervisors on the second and third shifts, and the major role of the area managers, as the supervisors on the first shift are called, is to act as facilitators of the teams' needs. Clearly power has been shifted to the work force.

The steel company was in the process of installing a state-of-the-art continuous casting process run with a multilevel computer system. Because of the problem of breakdowns and their enormous cost, management wants the operators of the equipment to be able to diagnose malfunctions and perform the maintenance required. It therefore is using a sociotechnical approach with work teams, job rotation, and skill-based pay. Despite initial trepidation, the union negotiated the necessary collective bargaining adaptations.

The operators received training in new skills, including preventive maintenance. The new process was in an early stage of implementation at the time of our visit, and there was apprehension among the workers, but those interviewed indicated that they wanted the greater responsibility: operators can stop production if there is a problem, and there is teamwork between bargaining unit people and supervisors rather than, as one worker put it, a "them vs. us" attitude. The workers find the approach both frightening and challenging; one stated, "You have to think for yourself."

A second aspect of this new approach to work organization relates to compensation. Unlike the rest of American manufacturing, there are no hourly workers in the synthetics and cable plants; everyone is salaried. Also, atypically, people are not paid for the particular job that they may be performing. In the cable plant, pay is based on the number of skills one has mastered and thus the different jobs one can perform.

Training also falls within the purview of the work teams in the cable plant. In the synthetics plant, the systems technician handles most of the training of the production assistants, and in both categories, workers rotate among the various jobs.

Training for Sociotechnical Systems

Plants moving toward sociotechnical system approaches to work organization have an added dimension in training needs. Switching from a highly structured organization with strict superior-subordinate relationships to one of autonomous teams is not easy. Employees at all levels and in all departments must be trained for the new way of operating or failure is likely.

Before retraining can begin, employees who may not fit into the new arrangement must be identified, for there is evidence that some people need a highly structured environment and react negatively to a situation in which their duties are not clearly spelled out and they are not closely supervised. This appears to apply to a small number of workers, however; most individuals relish the freedom and responsibility thrust on them. Even so, they must be trained in sociotechnical techniques, especially socially interacting all the time with fellow workers and supervisors on the basis of equality.

The steel mill that was simultaneously introducing both a completely new technology and a sociotechnical work system faced retraining problems at both the supervisory and production worker levels. The employees were a heterogeneous group. They covered the age and service gamut of people in their fifties with many years of service to those in their twenties with a short period of service; their ethnic backgrounds were highly diverse; and they came from different geographic areas. The younger, technically educated people were the most adaptable to the change, but overall, there were no insurmountable retraining problems, even with the diversity of the population.

Line management and human resources cooperated in developing selection tests, with a good deal of help from the employees doing the jobs, on the skills that were required. Agreement was reached with the union on such matters as which workers were to be kept in the operation and what duties the jobs actually would encompass. Employees could apply to work in this area or two others. Those eligible were sent an information booklet explaining sociotechnical concepts, the manning philosophy, the new equipment, and the new jobs. Those who remained interested went on to testing. Seventy percent passed the qualifying tests, and there were no equal employment problems or union concerns (that is, no disparate impact).

There was further orientation for those who had passed the examination, and then individuals were slotted into jobs. Employees could choose the jobs they wanted based on the order of their selection, with the highest priority going to those who would be displaced by the new processes. Workers transferring to casting from other departments kept reversion rights up to a certain level of training. After that, if they dropped out, voluntarily or otherwise, they fell into the labor pool.

Management wanted to train employees to be more proficient and more versatile, thereby enabling it to reduce manning levels. The question concerned whether operators could be retrained to do preventive maintenance, thereby reducing the size of maintenance crews. Human resources was involved in the development of the training program, but once it was underway, it was turned over to operating management, as subject matter experts, for execution. Of the $230 million spent on innovation, $10 million went into training, a ratio consistent with training costs for new projects in the industry.

Training got underway at least three, and for many workers, as long as eight months ahead of start-up. The first week of the program was devoted to orientation to the sociotechnical system, which was designed to gain further commitment to it. This was followed by twelve to thirteen weeks of generic maintenance training, interspersed with more information on the new process and on mechanical skills. Testing was conducted after each unit of training; an individual had to pass in order to go on to the next unit. Of the people who started, 16 percent dropped out, about half of them for lack of commitment, one-quarter due to inability to learn, and the other quarter of their own volition. Twenty percent of the surviving group required remedial training. An individual who failed a test went back for six and a half hours of remedial instruction and was then retested. One overall problem of the training program was the decline in employee excitement about the new jobs ahead, particularly the greater responsibility to be afforded them, as weeks of classroom study increased.

The first group to go through retraining was from metallurgy, and they had the highest failure rate, with only ten of sixteen completing the program. Fear of failure, in turn, led to the problem of maintaining the level of commitment to the retraining. But experience shows that the first group has the toughest problem. As it goes through the program and then returns to the plant floor and tells the second group about the retraining, that group is better prepared psychologically and has an easier time. Also the trainers learn from the experience of the first group and readjust the program to reduce the strains on the workers. Consequently the success rate for completing the training rose progressively.

There were particular stresses among the supervisors. First, they were in a new environment, isolated from the work site. Second, they were thrown into a new group, unfamiliar in many cases with one another. Third, since no new titles had been assigned yet, each supervisor was concerned with where he or she would stand in the new setup. Finally, they had the most serious problems of transition to the sociotechnical approach since they were used to working in a rigid environment with tight parameters. By taking the group to Japan for a month to see how the new technology operated, management was able to break down the barriers among the supervisors, who learned that a diversity of people must work together for the efficient operation of the equipment.

Another plant that has been utilizing the sociotechnical approach to work organization for ten years spends $1,000 annually per employee for training in specific skills, communications skills (conducted by the local university), and teamwork skills. The skills training falls within the purview of the autonomous work teams; on any given process, a senior operator is in charge of both production and training another person. Evidence that the newly trained worker is competent to perform the job is determined by examination.

The autonomous team approach to the organization of work has had tremendous impact on organizational structure. The teams assume most of the functions assigned to foremen in traditional plants, and layers of management have been eliminated (see figure 9–1). In the steel operation, the manning requirements came in even lower than had been expected as a result of reduced need for traditional maintenance workers.

The reactions of both managers and workers to this way of organizing work were positive. An area manager in the cable plant, with many years of experience in traditional environments, stated, "I always knew that there had to be a better way to run a plant and now I've found it." A worker on the shop floor said, "I like this setup because there is no boss breathing down my neck and no union restricting what I can do."

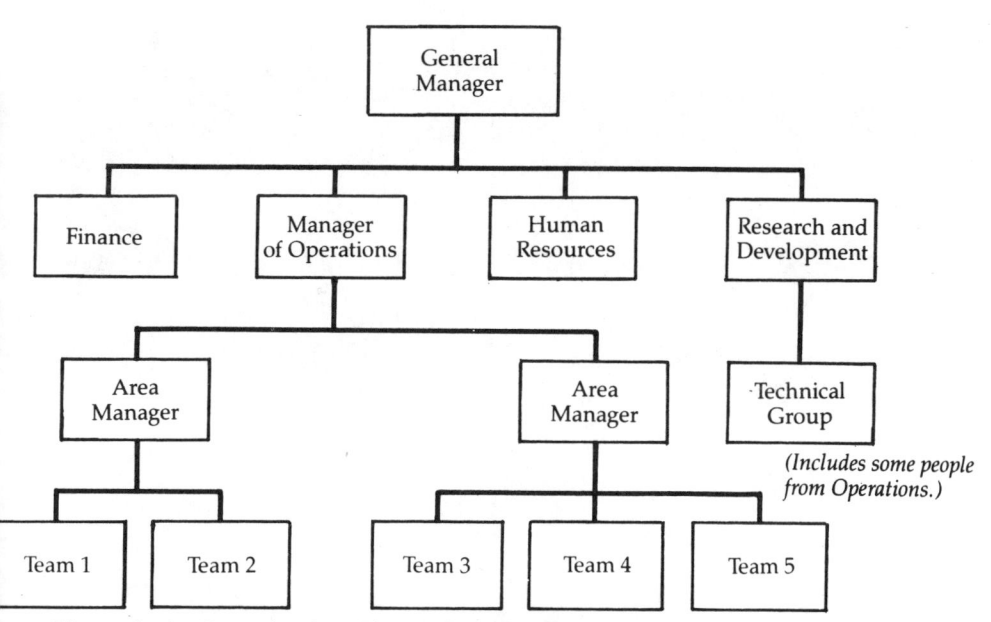

Figure 9–1. Organization Chart of Cable Plant Using Sociotechnical Approach to Work Organization

10
Organization and Management Structure

Plant Departmental Organization

Full-scale computer-integrated flexible manufacturing will upset traditional organization structure, but organization is being affected even now. Industrial plants are structured along departmental lines, with each department in charge of a discrete function as production moves from one to the other. In CIM, the objective is to achieve continuous production by centralizing machinery into work centers. When production is organized in this way, an entire product may be manufactured without being transferred from department to department.[1] Thus new technology cuts across the responsibilities of existing organizational units, requiring much greater interdepartmental cooperation or the redrawing of jurisdictional lines of authority.

Interdepartmental cooperation is not easy to achieve. In one case, top management is attempting to foster it by making 54 percent of the items in managerial performance rating common to all managers; in other words, they are being judged on the overall performance of the plant. As a result, greater vertical integration has been achieved. There is a more cooperative relationship among the sections of the organization, particularly since they must respond more quickly to problems. In disputes among departments, manufacturing engineering acts as a referee and information source.

Recognizing that technological change affects plant organization, another company has provided some direction from the corporate level, but each plant handles its own problems. Therefore a number of approaches to foster greater integration, including horizontal, vertical, and matrix, are used in this company. Another technique is the building of self-contained modules. They are often set up as separate departments, but some are woven into the traditional structure.

Not only are the distinctions among line departments blurred, but CIM also requires interaction between line and staff departments. The aim is to tie CAM into CAD, and with CAD/CAM, the division between design engineering and manufacturing virtually disappears. Both share the same data base, necessitating interaction between engineering and manufacturing. At this point, however, many companies are confronting the lack of a common data base, preventing the emergence of a true CAD/CAM system.

At one plant, a change in organizational structure that has emerged has been the creation of a new unit, CAM Systems Engineering. It is part of manufacturing engineering and is responsible for high-level maintenance of the plant's entire automated system, software maintenance, training with respect to the new technology, and identification of opportunities for systems improvement.

Although companies are having problems in affecting a plantwide integrated CAD/CAM system, they are having more success in the toolroom. As one person put it, "In the toolroom, CAD/CAM has become a way of life." Molds and dies are being designed by computer. Quality, cost of production, and the time required to produce a prototype have improved substantially. Toolmakers and engineers work together to improve designs. If a tool wears out, it is duplicated by taking out a tape and rerunning it.

A major theme stressed by most companies is the effect of manufacturing considerations on product design. "Design for automation" is the dictate. For example, if a part to be assembled contains many elements to be screwed into it, then using a robot would be uneconomical since a human can do that kind of work more efficiently. If the part were redesigned, however, so that the elements could be clamped in in one motion, a robot would be more efficient. The need to break down the traditional barriers between design engineering and manufacturing is obvious. It is no longer a matter of engineering tossing its design over the wall and saying to manufacturing, "Now go make it."

For some companies, designing for automation goes well beyond the idea of merely designing a product for automatic assembly; they think instead in terms of CIM. According to John A. White of Georgia Institute of Technology, "From a systems standpoint, it means designing the product so that a whole range of functions can be performed automatically: design changes, procurement, manufacturing assembly, handling, storage, control, packaging, testing, and so on."[2]

Organization at one company is taking a flexible shape, with an emphasis on teams composed of members from different departments analyzing problems. Interdepartmental barriers are breaking down, aided by the fact that the people who design a product follow it through production. At the same time, some centralization of structure is occurring. There are plants within a plant, but a centralized materials-handling system ties everything together.

Because the key to flexible automation is that a product must be designed for it, companies are putting people from engineering on the plant floor to work with the production people. In one case in which engineering was merged into production, the engineers' lack of human relations skills led to such protests by the union that the experiment was abandoned. Although sharp divisions between line and staff cannot be maintained, working out new relationships is not easy.

CIM and even CAD/CAM are today more concepts than reality. Software problems have hampered the ability of the various pieces to communicate with each other. It is reported that of the 40,000 programmable devices on GM's plant floors, only 15 percent are now able to communicate beyond the immediate process.[3] In order to solve this problem, GM has evolved the manufacturing automation protocol (MAP), a project to set standards for the communication bridges between pieces of equipment. IBM and other computer manufacturers also have agreed on steps to permit communication among computers made by different companies.[4] Digital Equipment Corporation (DEC), moreover, has begun to market a group of new, easily connected products, as well as a hardware and software kit permitting users of IBM PCs to retrieve data from DECs VAX computers.[5]

Factory organization will change considerably as flexible manufacturing systems begin operation. All departments—engineering, manufacturing, scheduling, finance, purchasing, and marketing—will have to be integrated into a unified whole because a master production schedule dictates the movement of production through its various phases, the adjustment of parts inventories, and the purchase of materials. All procedures will have to be standardized, with individual departments losing their exclusive control of pieces of the operation. For example, the ability of programmable automation to produce a batch of one with virtually no setup time allows the use of just-in-time inventory practices. This in turn affects materials purchasing, transportation, cash management (accounting), materials handling, sales, warehousing, and just about every other function in a plant.

New Ways of Managing

The management of industrial organizations is changing. The typical seat-of-the-pants decision making by managers is giving way to planning decisions based on the information provided by the CAD/CAM system. Middle managers and foremen feel threatened as they see the "little black books," through which they had exercised control over operations, being made obsolete. Abandoning their informal systems of operation and learning to conform with the unitary system is difficult for many of them. Managers must learn to conceptualize an entirely new way of operating and managing a people-process integrated system. Instead of acting as watchdogs and disciplinarians, they must become planners, trainers, and communicators.[6]

Managers at all levels must learn to operate in a horizontally decentralized organization in which people outside a unit participate in its decision making.[7] This means that managers spend more time interacting with each other and less in directing subordinates. The entire ethos of management is shifting from the traditional emphasis on the hierarchical chain and unity of command to a more open, organic style of organization.

Although most of the talk about new technology focuses on its impact on blue-collar workers, it is the managerial-supervisory group that is being most affected. Companies are following a variety of routes in attempting to help supervisors unable to make a satisfactory transition to their new roles. One technique used to overcome supervisory resistance to change is to try to convince the foreman that the new technique was his idea; if that can be done, he accepts it. Experience indicates, however, that new ideas cannot be imposed on supervisors. Where possible, obsolete supervisors have been transferred to older types of operations, retired early, or moved back into the production worker ranks, but some of them have been dismissed. One electrical products plant found that it needed an entirely new type of supervisor—one combining human resource skills with technical ability. After an unsuccessful attempt at using technically trained people, plant management hired college graduates with human resource skills and with the potential for learning enough of the required technical knowledge. They usually had liberal arts or social science degrees but were also familiar with mathematics and computers.

Another company that explicitly recognized the changed role of supervision undertook intensive retraining to help supervisors to become advisers, communicators, and effective team builders. The objectives of its training program were:

To improve the first-line managers' ability to manage people, manage systems, and manage change in increasingly complex and turbulent organizations.

To prepare first-line managers to meet the demands of a changing work force marked by younger, better educated employees who demand and expect more participation in the nature of their work.

To improve the first-line managers' knowledge and understanding of the plant mission so their role and responsibilities can fit with the mission.

To improve the fit between the first-line managers' role and their behavior in that role and the manufacturing strategy of the plant.

To raise the status, sights, and expectations of first-line supervisors to those of first-line managers.

To recognize training and development of first-line managers as an individual plant responsibility and an ongoing process.

To help identify the business and manufacturing system issues that block first-line managers in performing their jobs.

To improve the skills of first-line managers at analyzing and helping solve organizational problems.

To promote more open communication at all levels of management.

Experience at this company indicates that it is possible to transform old-line bosses into the new type of supervisor. Not only retraining but continuing education and careful selection of new supervisors become especially important.

The problem also must be seen from the supervisors' point of view. One of those interviewed said that supervisors lose identity and status with the introduction of advanced technology. A paticular difficulty arises when some young, well-educated subordinates have greater understanding of computer-controlled processes than their supervisors. Clearly companies must be careful to keep supervisors' technical abilities at least on a par with those of their subordinates.

Another company reported that as a result of advanced technology, its engineers train operators in the new processes directly on the shop floor. The supervisors, however, know only how to turn machines on and off and no longer are of much help in dealing with problems. They no longer schedule work, since that is done by computer, so now they are largely troubleshooters. Before automation, the job of supervisor was more manually oriented. The foreman had to do more legwork and supervise the flow of work. Now he receives a report that locates the work. The operators have actually received more training in computer and machine skills than their foremen. Despite these problems, the company never had to terminate existing supervisors; instead it moved them to operations that they were capable of handling.

In summary, few solutions for the managerial problems that accompany programmable automation appear to be readily evident. If companies want to move ahead with the new technology, they must begin to pay much closer attention to their managerial and supervisory ranks. In the long run, however, the span of control will increase considerably, and there will be relatively fewer supervisors.

Open Organization

Clearly a revolution in the organization of industrial enterprises is afoot. Layers of management are being stripped away, decision making is being pushed down the scalar chain, and work is being redesigned to be more meaningful. The movement can be described as a movement from a mechanistic to a more organic structure.[8]

The mechanistic structure, which had become typical of the large, bureaucratic company, was compatible with a situation of stable markets and stable technology. It was characterized by highly specialized and separate jobs, coordination by a hierarchic supervisory authority, knowledge concentrated at the top of the hierarchy, primarily vertical integration, and work behavior governed by supervisors' communications.

Such a system worked from the advent of mass production until recently. Its breakdown is related to changes in the world economy. Industrialization has spread from its original European–North American base to almost every corner of the globe. Less-developed nations with cheap labor enjoy comparative advantage in the production of labor-intensive products. At the same time, the process of technological diffusion has quickened, and many more nations today can compete in the manufacture of capital- and technologically intensive goods. With the slowdown in the world economic growth that began with the quadrupling of energy prices in 1973, productive capacity in many industries has outrun product demand. Also, affluent consumers seek greater product variety. These changes mean that markets are no longer stable. With the advent of programmable automation, technology also is not stable.

The organic structure, with its inherent flexibility, is more adaptable to a situation of rapidly changing markets and technology. It is characterized by greater decentralization, coordination by mutual adjustment, knowledge located anywhere regardless of authority, lateral flow of information, and communication in the form of information and advice. A constantly changing environment demands a large range of responses from the organization. In such situations, it is beneficial for each element to possess more than one function since each function may be performed in different ways with different combinations of elements. This need is being reflected in the expanding scope of jobs and the greater autonomy afforded those performing the jobs. Information systems should be designed to supply information to the point at which it is acted on. This need is reflected in the relocating of decision making further down the hierarchical structure. The organic structure can deal more effectively with uncertainty, which characterizes the manufacturing environment today and is likely to do so for the foreseeable future.

The mechanistic and organic structures are ideal models; no company is entirely one or the other. In fact, they can be viewed as two poles, with companies being somewhere along the continuum between them on the various factors characterizing each model (figure 10–1).[9] Until recently, most manufacturing companies were much closer to the mechanistic pole; they are moving toward the organic as the environment in which they operate becomes more uncertain. This is the revolution in organizational structure that is taking place. The requirements of programmable automation are reinforcing the need for flexibility, leading to a greater diffusion within industry of the new forms of organization.

Organic Organization   **Mechanistic Organization**

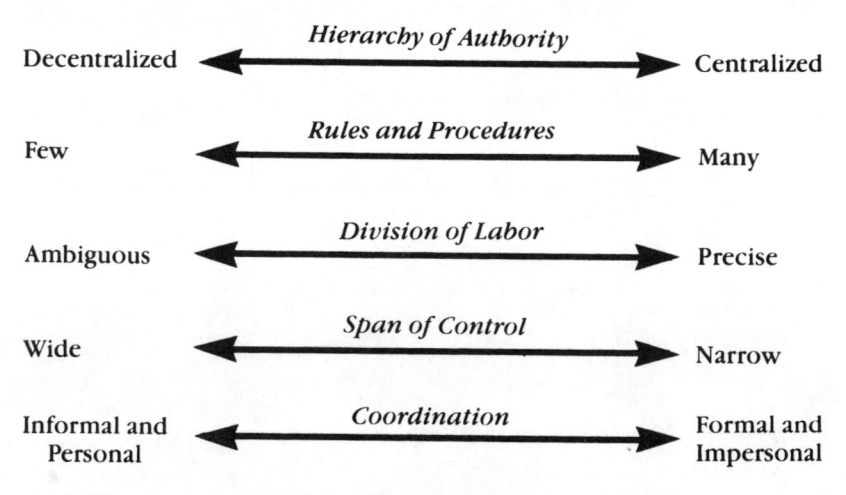

Organic		Mechanistic
Decentralized	← *Hierarchy of Authority* →	Centralized
Few	← *Rules and Procedures* →	Many
Ambiguous	← *Division of Labor* →	Precise
Wide	← *Span of Control* →	Narrow
Informal and Personal	← *Coordination* →	Formal and Impersonal

Figure 10–1. Continuum of Organizational Design Strategies

11
Union Responses

The profound change in the structure of industrial relations in the United States in the past two decades is well illustrated by the contrast between IRC's research with respect to hard automation and its study of the effects of computer-based technologies. When conducting the former research in the early 1960s, the overwhelming majority of manufacturing establishments studied were organized, and we had to search for some nonunion experience. In our current research, however, only half the facilities visited were organized. A number of unions, however, were represented: UAW, Clothing and Textile (ACTWU), Brotherhood of Electrical Workers (IBEW), International Union of Electrical and Electronic Workers (IUE), Machinists (IAM), Molders (IMWA), Steelworkers (USA), and Teamsters (IBT). (There also was an assortment of unions with small bargaining units covering ancillary workers, such as masons, plant guards, pattern makers, data processors, and operating engineers.)

Another significant difference between the two periods lies in the nature of the labor-management relationship. Earlier, that relationship was more adversarial. Also there has been a concomitant shift in bargaining power. In the 1960s, the unions were making a number of demands related to new technology; in the 1980s, employers are equally active in seeking changes in collective bargaining agreements because of new technology. These differences are linked to the weakened position of unionism, which in turn is related to employers' loss of market power stemming from intensified domestic and international competition.

Decline in union strength nationally, however, cannot be equated with a loss of power in any particular labor-management relationship. To the contrary, a number of employers continue to confront unions that can thwart their desires for greater efficiency. That this has not happened more often is due less to a union's inability to inflict damage on a company than to a recognition by union leaders that their members would suffer from such behavior. "For a high-wage economy like the United States, restoring competitiveness requires increased innovation and greater capital per workers; otherwise real wages would decline."[1] One full-time union official interviewed recognized this explicitly and said the only choice the union had was to agree to a reduction in wages and benefits or to work with new technology to enable the employer to compete better in the marketplace. His union eschewed the route of concessionary bargaining and chose instead to go along with computerized technology.

Thus the most important finding in the labor-management area is an almost total absence of union resistance to technological change. Effective communications programs, including long advance notice of impending innovation, have convinced employees and unions that computer-based technology is necessary to make the firm competitive and thus enable it to provide jobs for the bulk of its present work force. In the vast majority of cases, moreover, there have been no layoffs due to new technology, thus lessening union fears of it.

We discovered no difference in management's ability to introduce new technology between union and nonunion establishments. The advantage of nonunion plants, however, is the greater ability to effect organizational changes necessary to utilize programmable automation best. While unions have been amenable to the introduction of new technology, they have been more resistant to changing work rules to permit more flexible work force utilization. Even in these areas, however, some progress has been achieved.

To understand the greater difficulty in negotiating work rule changes, one must recognize differences between national and local unions. National union leaders generally have a broader perspective and are more familiar with the problems facing employers. Local leaders, whose experience is confined to one plant, cannot acquire the overall picture of the industry that national officers have, and so they often do not see the need to change existing policies. Labor-management relations at the local level also are often much more antagonistic than at the national level, with workers resentful of what they regard as mistreatment and autocratic behavior on the part of plant management. Although management is becoming less autocratic, local leaders are not sure that the change is permanent, and they remain leery of altering existing work practices.

Even when local leadership has been aware of the need to adjust to new situations, if often is constrained from reaching accommodation because of fear of rank-and-file opposition. In one case, a local union's agreement to work rule revisions did lead to the rise of a faction opposed to the existing leadership. Since rule changes must be negotiated at the plant level, these local union attitudes act as a barrier to achieving the necessary adaptations.

Changes are coming, albeit slowly, in plant labor-management relations. Union stewards are beginning to learn to take steps to avoid problems rather than simply try to solve them after they have arisen. At a plant that had introduced CNC machines with robot arms for feeding them, the chief shop steward sold the membership on accepting the machines and the work rule changes necessary for their effective utilization.

Management can help to train union officials for this new role. At the same time, plant management is becoming less directive and more willing to consult with union officers. One company that historically worked almost exclusively with the national union is working much more with the local leadership.

Labor-Management Conflict

People have been wrestling with the ramifications of technological progress for hundreds, if not thousands, of years. Farmers had to adjust to a new agricultural economy created by mechanized farm equipment, and industrial workers had to adjust to the demands of the factory. In the 1950s and 1960s, industrial workers and their unions grappled with the economic implications of hard automation, and now they must do so with programmable automation.

Programmable automation, like its technological ancestors, has an unsettling effect on the relationship between management and labor because it alters the nature of work and eliminates some job categories. Technological change also can threaten the viability of unions. Reductions in employment, even if accomplished through attrition, cut the union membership. In one case, a union local faced extinction as a result of external technological change. The production and maintenance workers at the plant belonged to a major industrial union, but there was also a small local of masons covering the refractory jobs, largely relining furnaces. In recent years, however, plastic-lined furnaces have been replacing traditional refractories. As a result, the number of mason jobs is declining. The union continues to hold jurisdiction over furnace jobs, but the masons, as craftsmen, are loath to perform the relining of the new furnaces, regarding the work as semiskilled and beneath them. Eventually the work may go to members of the production and maintenance unit, with the masons' local disappearing.

There are disagreements within management on the best strategy to pursue in effectuating the work practices changes needed to ensure optimum utilization of new technology. A few labor relations people, particularly those dealing with hard-nosed local union leadership, take the position that it may be better to act unilaterally by instituting desired change and letting the union grieve. The vast majority, however, adhere to negotiating with the unions and reaching agreements with them before proceeding. Given the nature of the bargaining process, following the latter strategy sometimes means granting quid pro quos for union acquiescence to work rule changes. In one case, in return for union agreement on the testing of applicants for jobs on new processes, management sweetened the retirement formula. Although the two issues were not directly related, the union took advantage of the situation to obtain something it had long wanted.

While labor leaders may share management's view on the need for technological innovation, they do not necessarily agree with management on what actions are required to accommodate the new technology and who should have to bear the cost associated with these actions. Management's objective is to operate the new technology as efficiently as possible; reduced manning schedules and relaxed work rules are critical to that goal. Organized labor's objectives are to protect members' jobs, the well-being of workers on those jobs, and the union's viability. The successful introduction of new technology into the workplace hinges on the parties' ability to resolve the conflicts that emerge from their competing interests.

Unions are concerned with such matters as which workers will be affected by new technology, what will happen to them, and who will staff the new processes. In many cases, moreover, workers in departments other than the one undergoing innovation are affected. At a steel complex introducing computerized continuous casting, the integration of the production process eliminated the need for a train crew to transport material to the unit. In almost all instances, these issues are worked out amicably by the parties, but some become areas of controversy.

One area of controversy often referred to in the literature on programmable automation is computer monitoring of work performance. The IAM, for example, has urged its locals to negotiate safeguards against the use of computers for time study, monitoring of workers, discipline, and job pacing.[2] Our research, however, uncovered only one plant in which this had become an issue between management and labor. Even in this instance, the union objection was not to monitoring but to the availability of the information, and the issue was resolved by placing consoles displaying work performance data on the shop floor, ensuring that both management and the union had the same information.

Organized labor has not mounted resistance to the new technology, but areas of conflict do exist that should not be discounted as challenges to management. These center on traditional union concerns—seniority systems, bargaining unit work and union jurisdiction, manning requirements, compensation, and economic security—and employers have adopted a variety of strategies to resolve them or at least minimize their intensity.

Seniority

Traditional seniority systems can be an impediment to the efficient operation of programmable automation. Their bumping provisions, which allow a senior worker to take the job of a junior worker when the former loses his or her job, undermine an employer's ability to place and keep the most qualified workers on the new technology and make it difficult to maintain a stable skills bank and a flexible work force.

Seniority systems can prove problematic whether they are broadly or narrowly defined. When the seniority unit is large—plantwide, for example—bumping provisions are troublesome because a worker with one type of skill can displace a worker at a job in a different department that demands a different set of skills. When the sensiority unit is narrow—departmentwide, for example—an employer may be frustrated in its efforts to redeploy senior workers who are displaced by technology because they cannot bump junior workers outside their seniority unit.

The companies resolved seniority-related problems in a variety of ways. Many unions are loath to agree to changes in the seniority provisions of collective bargaining agreements. Nevertheless, some companies were able to negotiate changes with the unions, while others took alternative routes.

An aerospace electronics manufacturer found that its plantwide seniority structure was proving disruptive to its efforts to keep trained workers on computer-based equipment during layoff periods. It responded by instituting a six-month freeze on jobs. In that period, no new workers could be brought into a unit, and no one could be laid off or transferred to another unit. The company preferred to carry excess workers on its paryoll than continually train workers on programmable automation.

An automotive components producer found that it could not keep trained operators on the robotic mold dipping process because of continual bumping. It was unsuccessful in persuading the union that adjustments to the seniority system were necessary, so the company began to use salaried technicians to run the equipment. At this point, the union agreed to take the jobs out of the bumping sequence in order to have the work remain in the bargaining unit.

At a railroad equipment manufacturer, after a three-week strike, the parties negotiated a variety of provisions designed to improve the operating efficiency of new CNC machines. One of the provisions created a new position, numerical control machinist (NCM), responsible for operating the CNC machines. The company was worried about the impact of liberal bumping language on its ability to maintain a cadre of trained NCMs and negotiated a provision that only workers skilled in all the operations performed by the equipment—boring, reaming, and drilling—could bump into the NCM classification. The company feels this will protect its investment in training NCMs and avoid the need for redundant training.

Seniority systems not only make it difficult to keep trained workers at jobs requiring special skills but also diminish an employer's ability to put the most qualified person in a job. This is particularly troublesome in a CIM environment because the equipment is so expensive and the cost of downtime so high.

An appliance manufacturer was concerned because seniority provisions were placing poorly qualified and less willing workers on computer-based equipment. The company's solution to the problem was to explain the jobs' demands and requirements in great detail to all eligible bidders for the openings. Those who were fearful of their ability to perform at the new jobs, often the most senior workers, withdrew from consideration.

Several companies have addressed this problem by requiring bidders for job openings to pass qualification tests—written examinations or demonstrations of skills and abilities. Unions, however, often resisted, believing that the tests did not effectively capture an employee's potential job performance.

In one facility in which automation has led to job upgrading, the senior qualified individual requesting a position always has gotten it. Management never has tried to promote a less senior person, even when, in its judgment, the person had superior ability to perform the job. As a result, the union has taken a more positive attitude toward technological change and has not tried to impede it. At the same time, no unqualified person has been advanced since basic ability must be demonstrated by passing tests.

At another plant, the fact that the senior employees always got the jobs on new technology caused serious problems because some of them turned out to be poor operators. Even training could not remedy the situation. In fact, seniority determines who is to be trained to work on automated equipment, although management believes that the major criteria should be ability and willingness to learn. The union, however, was unrelenting on seniority, and management was unwilling to press the issue to confrontation, particularly since the local had recently conceded to a significant reduction in the number of job classifications. Plant management recognized the political nature of a union and that consequently there were limits to the concessions the local leadership could negotiate without provoking membership opposition.

A steel company decided that qualification testing was necessary and mounted an intensive campaign to educate union leaders about the value and validity of testing. The company ultimately persuaded the union that only the most qualified could efficiently operate its multilevel computerized casting system, and the parties cooperated to develop a workable program. The workers themselves helped to determine the skill requirements for the new jobs. One of the most important features of the testing program is that those who failed to qualify received counseling on why they failed and had the opportunity to retake the test for the position when a new opening occurred.

A major union concern in the steel mill was the fate of senior workers who cannot qualify for jobs on the computerized equipment because they lack the requisite skills. The union believes these people should be considered permanently displaced and eligible for severance pay or enriched early retirement packages. Its position is that if management wants a smaller unit with fewer job classifications, it must take proper care of the displaced workers. The company has not conceded that such employees are eligible for these benefits.

Job Classifications

The greatest advantage of programmable automation is the flexibility in manufacturing that it permits; this requires greater flexibility within the work force. Individual workers must have a broader range of responsibilities and duties. By contrast, the minute division of labor ushered in with mass production made jobs precise, resulting in a multiplicity of classifications and wage rates. Although management introduced this system of work organization, with the coming of industrial unionism fifty years ago, it was codified into labor-management agreements. Companies that have labor agreements with narrow job classifications restricting the tasks that individuals may perform often are frustrated in their attempts to achieve optimal manning levels. Employers therefore have been attempting to modify classification systems by broadening jobs. Unions generally resist management's efforts to broaden jobs because they believe job security for members is diminished.

One of the most common areas of conflict centers on management efforts to have operators perform minor maintenance, particularly since this often leads to jurisdictional disputes with maintenance, which seeks to preserve the integrity of existing craft demarcations. The problem, particularly acute when production and maintenance workers are represented by different unions, can lead to many grievances. Even so, some managements have concluded that the advantages of broadening operators' responsibilities outweigh the labor relations difficulties.

At the steel plant, management was determined to man its state-of-the-art computerized casting equipment as efficiently as possible. This meant that operators would do minor maintenance. The company believed that, under the existing contract language, it could require this, and it was willing to go to arbitration to enforce this right, but it did not have to go that route. After long and arduous negotiation, the union ultimately agreed to broaden the operator classification to include minor maintenance duties, in part because it believed the new manning system would ultimately fail and the company would have to hire additional workers. The company noted that it would have to check closely that operators were indeed maintaining the equipment as well performing their production tasks.

Interestingly several companies indicated that their contracts permitted operators to do minor maintenance or allowed craftsmen to apply more than one skill but that supervisors found it less risky to wait for the most skilled worker, even if only nominal skills were required to correct the problem. At one company, a supervisor would wait for an electrician to repair a malfunctioning robot, though other tradesmen were available and capable of fixing it.

Since unions have built much of their job protection on existing classifications, they are reluctant to change them. Yet recognizing that the old system has become anachronistic and that their members desire to perform more meaningful work, they have been negotiating changes. Thus in many plants, the number of separate jobs is being reduced so that workers can perform a greater variety of tasks.

At an electronics manufacturing establishment, massive adjustments in the classification system were instituted, with concurrence of the union. The number of classifications was slashed from 160 to 40. Under the new system, jobs carry greater responsibilities, and they are more highly paid. The consolidation has improved management's flexibility to make work assignments, and, despite the higher wage rates for the expanded jobs, total labor costs have been reduced. For example, the old system called for assembler A, assembler B, and an entry-level classification. The parties were continually wracked by disputes concerning whether assembler A or B could do certain work. Under the new structure, the A and B classifications have been combined, and management can assign work with greater freedom, while many workers receive higher pay.

An office equipment manufacturer and an automotive company also negotiated broader jobs and fewer classifications. In the plant of the latter company, 125 separate classifications, including more than 20 for skilled tradesmen, were condensed into 25 production classifications and 8 skilled ones. Accomplishing that change required long and arduous negotiations before the local assented. Corporate headquarters reported that it encountered less union resistance to modifying job classification systems and effecting other necessary changes at those plants in which layoffs had occurred because of poor sales during the 1981–1982 recession. The dramatic reduction in job classifications at this plant was particularly noteworthy since its product line was not cyclically sensitive and no layoffs had taken place.

One technique for overcoming union resistance to broader classifications is to include work that was not previously in the bargaining unit in the expanded jobs. Generally this means including setup work, and the setup and operate classification is expanding. Workers like the greater responsibility. In one case in which management reorganized the production process so that people worked in teams and then made each team responsible for setting up its own work, it found that setup was performed better than when it had been the responsibility of the industrial engineering department.

Another type of job classification problem relates to what workers do when processes are being altered. At one company, it was typical for the production workers to be idle when the die presses were being changed, causing a significant increase in labor costs. To remedy the situation, management would run an excess line for production during the three shifts required to change dies. Now management is bringing in a $19 million transfer line, and there will be no excess line to be worked. The company's aim is to raise all the workers to the highest grade in the department and have them responsible for every job since dies will be changeable in a few minutes. Management had three options for accomplishing its goal: build a new plant, thus avoiding any negotiation with the union; use an old plant that had been closed and make the new arrangement a condition of reopening the plant; or negotiate the change of expanding jobs and training the workers. It chose the third way but still is a long way from successfully effectuating it.

Bargaining Unit Work

The changes technology is bringing to the nature of work are raising complex questions about whether a particular job belongs inside or outside the bargaining unit. Some factory workers are relying less on their traditional skills and tools and more on computers to perform their jobs, and employers are arguing that the nature of such work qualifies it for exclusion from the bargaining unit. Unions, fearing an erosion of the bargaining unit, counter that the work should remain a bargaining unit task.

At the companies visited, the issue was commonly resolved in favor of the union. At an electronics company, toolmakers were upgraded because they work with CAD equipment. The company said that although the work objectively qualifies for exclusion from the bargaining unit, management elected to maintain the status quo to avoid a confrontation with the union that might poison the existing atmosphere of cooperation.

At an automotive company, the problem related not to toolmakers but to the programming of industrial robots. Computer programming at the company has never been a bargaining unit task, but the union argued that bargaining unit employees should program the robots because the programmable automation is doing work formerly performed by represented employees. Here too the union was concerned about the erosion of the bargaining unit. The company relented and agreed that all work done within the bargaining unit before the change in technology would remain there after. Bargaining unit people do the on-line programming of machines. As the jobs of welders and spray painters are robotized, these workers do the programming of the robots, and electricians are responsible for their maintenance. Bargaining unit employees are also programming computers that control other forms of high technology, such as unmanned guided vehicles that carry materials throughout a plant. The company expressed concern, however, that its concession to include the programming of robots and other shop floor programmable automation as bargaining unit work will encourage the union to demand that all programming, including off-line work, be done by unit workers.

The question of programmable control of a machine remains in contention at this company. For example, an engineer formerly designed a circuit and then gave it to an electrician to wire. Now the engineer designs the circuit on a computer, pushes a button and it goes on tape, and only after that does he hand it to an electrician. The union contends that the engineer is wiring a circuit, which is bargaining unit work, and therefore the electrician should push the button. Management disagrees and the issue remains unresolved. Such issues, however, rarely go to arbitration, the parties preferring to work them out themselves.

In other industries the parties do resort to arbitration of bargaining unit work disputes. At the steel company that was introducing a continuous casting process controlled by three levels of computers, the issue of what work belonged in the bargaining unit was resolved through compromise along logical grounds. Level 1, computer control of individual machines, will be handled by electrical technicians, who are members of the bargaining unit. Level 2, computer control of the metallurgical process, will have some bargaining unit personnel plus engineers. Level 3, the overall process automation, will be run by non–bargaining unit personnel.

Even when the parties can resolve the question of whether a job belongs in the bargaining unit, there still remains the issue of which worker shall perform it. Does a particular task belong to an electrician or to a pipefitter? At one company, labor-management conflict has arisen over the matter of robot repair. The union says it belongs in the bargaining unit, but management disagrees. The issue is further confused because neither labor nor management knows which specific classification should perform the repair; within the bargaining unit, should it be the operator or the machinist, and among salaried personnel, should it be the programmer or the electronic technician?

The issue of who does the programming is a contentious one. In most plants, including nonunion ones, the task is assigned to separate units of programmers or to engineers, largely because most programming is done off-line but also in a few cases because management feared that the production workers would not be capable of doing it, at least not without considerable expensive training.

In unionized situations, the main management motivation, however, is to keep programming out of the bargaining unit, where it would be subject to stringent rules of demarcation and seniority bumping procedures. The seniority system intensifies those problems. Management would be more willing to train operators to perform on-line programming if it could count on those workers retaining those jobs. But if every time some change in the plant induced a series of job movements and someone new ended up with the job, management would face extraordinary training costs and inefficient operations.

Several of the companies reported that programmable automation was also generating jurisdictional disputes within and between unions. The nature of the new technology makes it possible for relatively unskilled workers to perform tasks that previously required specific skills. At an appliance plant, management wanted the operators to do minor maintenance to minimize machine downtime. Its goal was complicated by the fact that there were two bargaining units in the plant. The largest covered the mass of production and maintenance workers. Maintenance was not divided into separate crafts; there was only one classification, and these workers were responsible for electrical and mechanical maintenance. The toolroom, however, was a separate bargaining unit, organized by a different union, and these workers were responsible for all major repairs to equipment and processes.

Two jurisdictional disputes resulted. The production and maintenance workers represented by the same union were feuding because machine operators were doing minor maintenance work, such as replacing electronic modules, on their equipment. Despite the objections of its maintenance members, the production workers' union supported the company's action because it meant more work and job enrichment for its members. At the same time, maintenance workers represented by the production workers' union were battling with the toolroom maintenance workers. The toolroom workers' union was opposed to all moves to broaden maintenance duties of the production and maintenance unit. Since toolroom workers had responsibility for major repairs, their union felt that only they should have the right to work on the new technology. Management and the union that represents the bulk of the workers opposed that view. Management has reluctantly concluded that there is no good solution to the jurisdiction problems, short of job guarantees for everyone, which it is unwilling to extend. Management acknowledged that disputes will continue to arise, and they will be resolved on a case-by-case basis.

Compensation

Some unions are responding to employers' demands for broadened jobs with counterdemands for job upgrades and higher pay rates. Companies are upgrading jobs that have been expanded and raising pay levels accordingly. In one plant, all thirty workers in a plastic molding operation that had been automated were divided into autonomous work teams in which everyone could operate the system and keep it functioning by making minor repairs.

All differences in job title, duties, and pay were eliminated, and one new higher grade was established.

Companies are approaching this issue cautiously, however, and making pay adjustments only where they are objectively warranted. They are resisting the temptation to bump rates up merely to overcome union resistance to job classification changes. Companies that have moved to the team approach for staffing automated equipment generally institute a skills-based compensation structure, with workers paid higher rates as they acquire additional skills. The usual practice is to make the current highest rate the top rate obtainable under the skills-based structure.

One fascinating compensation issue that arose concerned the pay of workers who will be upgraded by new technology during the training period. In one case, the union argued that the training was so arduous, with a good deal of classroom study, that the higher rates should be paid during the training period. Management disagreed but conceded that the old rates also did not apply. It therefore established interim rates between the old and the new, but the possibility existed that the union might yet challenge them.

Computer-based automation is not only provoking management into modifying its basic pay structure but is compelling it to reconsider the merit of incentive systems. Several of the companies reported that programmable automation renders traditional individual incentive pay systems invalid because production and quality are controlled by a computer, not the workers. In many of these companies, however, individual incentive pay systems have become ingrained on the shop floor culture, and unions are resisting management's attempt to eliminate or modify them.

The inapplicability of individual incentive systems to computer-based equipment is particularly troublesome in a workplace that has only islands of automation. Workers may attempt to exercise seniority to transfer from computer-based equipment to conventional technology so they can qualify for incentive pay. This type of incentive problem complicated the introduction of CNC machining centers at one plant. Under the old technology, all jobs were incentive rated, but this was impossible with CNCs, and that was a factor in the labor-management dispute over their introduction. Even the resolution of the issue did not solve all management's problems. Workers accepted jobs on the CNCs, although they paid only time rates, because jobs were not plentiful on the old machines. Management feared that as business picked up again, the workers trained as CNC operators would exercise their seniority to bump back to their old jobs so that they could earn up to a 25 percent premium in pay.

Many companies are considering group incentives as an alternative to existing individual incentive programs. Some unions also favor forms of gain sharing, that is, group incentive plans through which the employees share the benefits of productivity gains as in, for example, Scanlon, Rucker, or

Improshare plans. A steel company faced a particular dilemma. The collective bargaining agreement stipulated that there were to be incentive rates, but management has been unable to devise individual incentives for the jobs affected by new technology. The contractual requirements and worker morale (under traditional technology, workers could earn as much as 35 percent more in incentive pay) put pressure on management to solve the problem, and it is exploring a gain sharing approach. An added advantage of the group incentive approach is that it not only overcomes the deficiencies of an individual system under programmable automation but also emphasizes the team orientation that is often critical to the effective operation of computer-based equipment.

Economic Security

Job dislocation often accompanies the introduction of computer-based equipment. Absent an increase in product sales, fewer workers are needed to produce the current level of output. In some cases, the dislocated worker can bump a junior worker and maintain employment. In other instances, the dislocated worker lacks sufficient seniority or appropriate skills and suffers job loss.

The respondents to the IRC questionnaire believed that strengthening job security for their members would be the first priority of union leaders. They were correct. Unions are extremely concerned about the job dislocation impact of the programmable automation and often demand some form of income or job security as a condition for cooperating with management on the implementation of the new technology. Several of the employers declined to extend any new form of economic protection to workers displaced by technology, either because of the expense or because they did not wish to set a precedent of providing support to displaced workers. Others have negotiated such measures with unions.

At a telecommunications company, workers dislocated by technological change are covered by two separate income maintenance plans. One provides pay rate protection for twelve months, or the life of the contract, whichever is greater, to those who must take lower-paying jobs within the organization as a result of changing technology. Technological change is defined as the introduction of manufacturing equipment different in nature or type from that previously utilized by the company or of substantial modifications to present manufacturing equipment. The other income protection program is a layoff allowance plan that makes payments on the basis of years of service to workers who are made superfluous for any reason, including technological change.

Some companies did not see the need for negotiated agreements designed to protect workers from layoffs because they are successfully redeploying displaced workers within their organizations. This is the position of an environmental controls manufacturer. The company is seeking to achieve employment stability and to that end is making more use of supplemental employees and shortened workweeks to minimize layoffs. Even so, it will not negotiate an employment security provision, believing that this would create false expectations since layoffs will continue to occur, as dictated by the business cycle. With respect to technological change, however, there have been no layoffs because management has been able to redeploy the work force. For example, when it automated the process of manufacture for one of its major products, it moved dislocated workers among the six facilities in a metropolitan area that comprise the bargaining unit. In one case, corporate headquarters, under the prodding of the human resources function, forced one division to absorb surplus employees from another as part of a deal for it to obtain the additional capital for capacity expansion. This company also said that it would relocate hourly employees if local redeployment was impossible. Other companies suggested they might do the same. Many managers, however, believe that hourly workers will not move along with the job unless there is no alternative in the local job market.

The greatest form of economic protection an employer can offer is job security. One company had agreed to provide this benefit to workers with at least one year of seniority who are displaced as a result of technological change, defined here as any change in product, methods, processes, or the means of manufacturing at a location. An employee who loses his or her job because of the introduction of new technology continues to draw normal pay but may be placed in a training program, replace some other worker being retrained, be transferred to another plant, or be placed in a nonbargaining unit job.

An office machine manufacturer also agreed to union demands for job security in an effort to cement union-management cooperation and achieve greater stability within the work force. Its plan, negotiated in 1983, provided job security for the life of the agreement to all employees on the payroll at the date of the signing. In exchange for the employment guarantee, the union acceded to greater flexibility in work force utilization and to the right of management to hire temporary employees, if needed, at lower rates of pay. That agreement was renewed recently. Under this job security arrangement, the company's potential economic burden diminishes over time as a result of normal attrition.

Even when there is no loss of employment in a plant, new technology can eliminate the jobs of particular workers. The easiest way to protect displaced workers is to transfer them to other jobs elsewhere in the plant, and most collective bargaining agreements contain elaborate provisions governing such transfers. A problem may arise when job classifications are narrow, for there may not be other jobs available in a displaced worker's classification. In a number of cases, unions have become aware of this problem, and the need to solve it has been one factor in the willingness to negotiate broader job classifications.

Some collective bargaining agreements require that workers displaced by new technology be transferred to other jobs that are comparable in compensation to their old ones. Often the workers require retraining in order to qualify them for similarly rated positions. When comparably rated jobs have not been available, transferred workers have been provided with protected rates. In a couple of cases, special local agreements extended the period of rate protection beyond that normally allowed.

It is not common to transfer bargaining unit employees to other plants even when there are insufficient jobs for displaced employees at their home plant. Some companies, however, give employment preference to workers displaced from any of their plants. If such a worker is hired at another plant, he or she retains seniority for pension and benefit purposes only. A few collective bargaining agreements do provide for interplant transfers, either because of transfer of work from one plant to another or displacement by new technology. Relocation allowances are provided in these cases. Interplant transfers, however, are virtually impossible when different unions represent the workers at a company's various plants.

In one case, a number of international unions representing the workers at different plants of a corporate division worked out an interplant transfer program. The coordinated bargaining committee of the unions and the division negotiated a job protection clause according to which workers laid off from one plant would be given preference for jobs for which they were qualified at another. They would be able to switch membership from one union to another too.

In another case, the acceptance of transfers by a large percentage of the workers displaced by a movement of work from an obsolete plant to a new one located elsewhere complicated labor-management relations. The local at the old site had been a thorn in the side of the national union as well as the company. At the new location, management wanted to inculcate a new set of attitudes. It pointed out to the workers that if the plant did not prove successful, there would be no where else for them to transfer. A carrot also was offered: if the plant did well, it might be expanded. Management's hopes were dashed. The entire local leadership transferred to the new facility. Even worse from management's point of view, it brought with it all the same local rules, including that requiring annual election of officers. As a result, the shop stewards are always electioneering, and there is a continuous turnover of union officers on the shop floor. Facing the need to be continually reelected, moreover, local officials are afraid to be seen as less than supermilitant.

The hard-nosed attitude of the union leadership presents management with other problems. Company policy is to encourage workers to learn more and broaden their capabilities, but at this plant, management has to be careful because new job responsibilities can lead to new issues in labor relations. For example, if workers are taught too much programming, the local will insist that programming the computers themselves, not just the robots, should be a bargaining unit task.

Even so, some progress in improving labor-management relations has taken place. One reason is the decided improvement in working conditions at the new plant compared to the old one; the new plant, for example, is air-conditioned. Joint labor-management committees have been formed to deal with many QWL issues (though there is no QWL program in existence), such as choosing a vendor for the plant cafeteria. On management's side, there is less directive supervision and more consultation with workers.

A sign of some improvement in labor relations is the reduction in the number of grievances as compared with the former site. Nevertheless, active grievances number 150, 50 more than management had wanted to achieve. Grievances keep coming in largely because the local is so politicized, but many are related to opportunities to work overtime and so are not serious problems. The problem that is serious, from management's point of view, is the local's continued rejection of QWL, which prevents employee participation in problem solving.

In the absence of a sufficient number of jobs, a major way to ensure some income security has been through early retirement, and this route was used in almost all cases, organized and nonunion. Both unions and management have favored special early retirement of older workers in preference to layoff of younger ones. Unions consider it more equitable, since the younger members keep their jobs and the older ones receive a measure of income security. Management prefers retaining younger workers, considering them more productive, and when jobs are altered by new technology, it can receive a greater return on its investment in retraining. Thus many collective bargaining agreements were amended to include more liberal early retirement provisions.

At one plant that suffered severe reductions in the size of the work force largely due to product market conditions but partially to the introduction of advanced technology in an attempt to stem market loss, early retirement was the major means of accomplishing that reduction. The collective bargaining agreement called for full pensions at age 60, but the parties amended it to permit retirement as early as age 55, at 72 percent of the full pension. Over the six-year period, 60 percent of the reduction of the work force was accomplished by retirement.

Employee Involvement

Employee involvement activities facilitate the introduction and efficient operation of programmable automation because they create an atmosphere of trust and credibility between labor and management and provide a forum for educating labor about the company's economic condition. This was true in both union and nonunion settings. Furthermore, employee involvement is a vehicle for obtaining workers' input on the proper design and operation of the new technology. Employers are finding that hourly workers, because of their intimate knowledge of the work process, can be of great assistance to engineers and others charged with developing and installing the new technology.

Management and union attitudes toward involvement vary greatly among companies and unions and even within a company or union. The initiative, however, always came from management, with unions responding favorably (usually), unfavorably, or halfheartedly. Those in the labor movement who are opposed to employee involvement see it merely as a vehicle to get the workers to view production from a managerial perspective and to co-opt the unions into acceding to management desires. These people continue to advocate an adversarial labor-management relationship, denying a connection between employer efficiency and employee welfare. This is a minority viewpoint, at least within the cases studied; employee involvement is spreading, even to the point of union acceptance of sociotechnical approaches to work organization.

At an office equipment manufacturer, employee involvement is carried out through quality-of-work-life circles and evolved from a long history of positive labor-management relations. In 1977, the labor contract stated the intention of having employee involvement, and the 1980 agreement formally established the circles. Today employee involvement permeates nearly every aspect of business activity. It has played an important role in helping the company successfully introduce CIM systems. Through the quality circles, employees become aware of competitors' costs and sensitive to the company's needs to improve production methods. The company believes that because union leaders and workers are more knowledgeable about the business, they are more willing to agree to contract changes that will help staff the technology more productively. This was the case in 1980 when the company and union negotiated a work rule change that permitted machine operators to perform minor maintenance duties. Hourly workers also work along with manufacturing and engineering personnel on teams that study how products can be designed for assembly by robots.

The company decided to install computer-based manufacturing systems because it urgently needed to reduce costs and improve product quality. Its market share had dropped precipitously in a relatively short period, and it was compelled to cut its hourly work force by over 50 percent. Against a backdrop of employment loss and continuing financial difficulties for the company, the union leadership supported the company's move to new production methods. In fact, it was reported that at times the union leadership called for the company to adopt new technology more quickly, believing that the step would serve the long-term job security interests of employees.

Despite the potential benefits of employee involvement to both managers and workers in a programmable automation environment, there is some resistance to such activities by both management and labor officials. At an automotive plant, management decided that it would run awareness meetings to help workers understand the company's reasons for introducing various pieces of computer-based equipment and to respond to workers' concerns related to the new technology. Although the national union supports QWL programs, the local union officials had run on a platform opposing them and declared that workers should not participate in them. Many workers disregarded the leadership's direction and attended the meetings on a voluntary basis. The company asked the national union to compel local union officials to support the employee involvement activities, but the national leaders said that although the union endorsed the company's programs, it could not force local acceptance.

It is not uncommon for national union leaders to be more supportive of management's technology improvement initiatives and programs such as employee involvement, which buttress them, than local union officials, probably because the negative political fallout that may result from job dislocations associated with new technology falls most heavily on local union officials.

A history of hostile labor-management relations at a plant makes local leaders suspicious of the company's motives, and it takes time and special efforts by management to engender new attitudes. General Electric, for example, has successful involvement programs at a number of plants but not at the one in Lynn, Massachusetts, long a center of stormy labor-management relations. Local union officials pulled out of a quality circle program, charging that authoritative management was merely being clothed in participative dress.[3] Furthermore, the union wanted shop floor discipline to be part of the circles' agendas, but management would not agree to that.

When involvement includes sociotechnical approaches with autonomous work teams, local union officials face the difficult problem of negotiating changes in the collective bargaining agreement that may be unpopular with some of the members: condensing multiple job classifications and blurring the distinctions between production and maintenance categories. In one case, the local leadership agreed to such changes only under the prodding of the international representative, for it then could blame the international if things did not work out well. It must be recognized that any type of employee involvement program holds risks for a union. When involvement does not succeed and when things go wrong, it is the local leaders whom the members blame. Indeed, employees too are at risk, since employee involvement can involve interpersonal conflict within the work group.[4]

At several of the companies, particularly those with a history of confrontational union relations, there was a conflict between those with labor relation responsibilities and those with broader human resources duties. When a financially troubled steel company with a forty-year history of adversarial union relations decided to introduce a computerized casting system, its human resources staff advised that the union be consulted. The labor relations staff opposed this idea, arguing that the union would ask questions that management could not answer. It also contended that the union should not be viewed as a collaborator on the project.

The project manager, after too long a delay by his own admission, told the union the company's plans and welcomed its participation. The union first resisted the employer's invitation, skeptical of the company's motives, but ultimately agreed to work with the company. Several agreements pertaining specifically to the technology were fashioned after an international union representative assumed responsibility for any negative results. The local union did, however, insist that the technology agreements be concluded well before the annual union officer elections. Several companies in the study reported similar requests from local union representatives.

Formal union-management employee involvement programs are not without risk to both parties. Unions fear being co-opted and workers' contributing to productivity increases that lead to their own displacement from jobs. For management, these programs can complicate local labor relations. In the experience of one company, although its QWL arrangement is supposed to be separate from collective bargaining, bargaining matters do creep in because of economic conditions. Even so, this company wants to extend QWL to all of its plants. QWL is a change agent, particularly in moving labor-management relations away from their traditional adversarial nature.

Management at one plant concluded that its new integrated manufacturing systems would not work unless the culture of the plant was changed. To that end, the union was fully informed and its involvement in the project for technological change solicited. The local agreed and became part of the project with union representatives—chief steward and the stewards of each of the production departments—on the planning committee. Meetings with employees were held regularly, and a much more cooperative industrial relations climate emerged.

This experience leads to an important general conclusion: a union will cooperate in employee involvement efforts only if there is a role for it; otherwise, the leadership will view employee involvement as an effort to undermine the union.

Nonunion Labor Relations

Because half the facilities in the study were not organized, some similarities and differences between unionized and nonunion ones with respect of new technology should be noted. First, a company's ability to introduce new technology at a plant is not affected by whether it is unionized. This stems not only from the fact that unions have not resisted technological change but also from the fact that more resistance to change has come from lower and middle managers than from shop floor workers. Indeed the only cases of worker sabotage of new equipment (both minor) that we uncovered occurred in an unorganized plant. In companies in which some plants are unionized and others are not, managers in the latter sometimes are reluctant to introduce new technology because they fear that change will upset the workers and make them more amenable to union organizing attempts. Overall, however, there was no difference in ability to introduce change regardless of union status.

Second, although there is little distinction in the ability to introduce technological innovation, there is a decided difference in management's ability to make other changes to facilitate the most efficient utilization of the technology. In unorganized situations with no third party, management is free unilaterally to alter manning schedules, shift work from one group of employees to another, combine jobs, and promote individuals.

Third, despite management's unilateral authority in nonunion operations, it has not abused its power in dealing with employees. To the contrary, nonunion companies and facilities have been responsible in their human resource policies. Wages and benefits of nonunion operations were at least comparable to those of unionized ones in the same industries. Similarly employees in unorganized situations have enjoyed as much job security as those unionized, and probably even more since some nonunion companies follow full employment policies and do not lay off regular employees. Where layoffs have occurred, nonunion facilities have adhered to the seniority criterion.

Finally, most nonunion plants provide employees with means of adjudicating disputes through internal appeals procedures. Some companies have elaborate two-way communications systems whereby workers can bring grievances to the attention of higher management if they are dissatisfied with the response from their own supervisors. In fact, managements often claim that effective communications are the key factor in maintaining nonunion status.[5]

A number of companies operated formal grievance procedures, with specific individuals empowered to act on behalf of employees; thus they played a role similar to that of the shop steward in unionized situations. In one plant, hot-line telephones, which workers could use to get an immediate response to a grievance, were available on the shop floor. Some companies have third-party arbitration of unresolved grievances; one has had such arbitration for four decades. In practice, however, there were few employee grievances related to new technology, and those that did occur invariably were settled without great travail.

Conclusions

One of the great ironies of industrial history is that all technological change tends to be viewed by the current generation as revolutionary, when in many cases it is evolutionary and therefore can be effectively managed with contemporary tools using recent history as a guide. Today programmable automation is characterized as revolutionizing the American workplace. Certainly there are elements of truth in this, but most management and union officials view the new technology as just the latest episode of change in a long and complex series of changes.

This is not to say that computer-based automation is not generating workplace changes special to its character. The important point is that employers often can successfully manage their conflicts with unions over computer-based technology with extensions of proved strategies, such as early employee communications and employee participation. With proper business planning, manpower management, and employee training, employers can overcome unions' greatest fears about the impact of technology on workers.

Changes in seniority structures, job classification systems, and compensation schemes may become necessary to exploit the new technology fully, and disputes will inevitably arise when management seeks to modify existing contract language. Employers must know the history of the workplace, strengths and weaknesses of managers, characteristics of the work force, economic climate, union political environment, and worker expectations and needs before they attempt to negotiate modifications to the labor agreement. The collective bargaining process is a proved way to resolve workplace conflict and should prevail as well when the source of conflict is technological change, especially since the parties have come to understand that their fates are intertwined.

In most cases, labor and management have moved toward less adversarial relationships. The greatest strides have been made in situations in which management has had communications programs that have kept unions fully informed on the need for, the nature of, and the impact of new technology. Managements have worked closely with the unions representing their employees, to the point of including union representatives on the committees planning the introduction of new processes. Although this was not true in the majority of unionized situations, employee involvement in planning for new technology was as prevalent in organized as in nonunion situations.

One case was remarkable because it represented the conversion of a hostile labor-management relationship into a cooperative one. Management recognized that its new integrated manufacturing system would not work unless the entire culture of the plant was changed. To that end, the union was fully informed and its involvement in the project for technological change solicited. The local agreed, and once it became part of the project, it was kept fully informed at all stages as to what was transpiring. Union representatives were on the planning committee, and meetings with employees were held regularly to report on progress and difficulties being encountered. Management's efforts paid off; a much more cooperative industrial relations climate emerged, evidenced by a dramatic 75 percent drop in time lost due to work stoppages. The new relationship has worked to the benefit of the union too. There are no signs of internal dissension, the leadership was easily reelected recently, and the union is represented on plant committees. The technological change has also led to improved product competitiveness and, thus, a recall of laid-off workers.

Another company, a manufacturer of diversified products, has established a strategy of actions for managers to follow in order to build strong factories:

1. Delineate management-leadership functions.
2. Manage the boundaries or frontiers.
3. Design responsibility into jobs.
4. Pay attention to the role of supervisors.
5. Make the union a partner.
6. Design more flatness into the structure.
7. Choose technology.
8. Keep the layout simple.
9. Write instructions for information systems in plain English.
10. Compensate to encourage learning and productivity.
11. Develop appropriate personnel policies and practices.
12. Realize the power of symbols.

Making the union a partner is one of its recommended actions. To that end, it encourages the formation of in-plant labor-management committees and has prepared material telling plant managers how to do so. It defines a labor-management committee as a group of union members and managers that meets periodically to identify and resolve issues of shared interest that normally fall outside the negotiated contract. Such committees should have equal management and union representation, with the former coming from the lower levels of management.

The in-plant committees should have cochairmen, one from the union and the other from management, and the position of chair should be alternated between the two groups. The stress is on consensual decision making rather than voting. There must be meeting agendas, but the committee should not get stalemated on controversial matters, but put them aside for the time being, if necessary, and move on to other issues. Minutes should be kept and published.

Although the labor-management committees function within the collective bargaining process, they deal with problems outside the contract. Their most important feature is mutual influence. If problems emerge that require contractual changes, they should be deferred to the next negotiations but with recommendations to the negotiating committee. It may also be wise in specific instances to agree to suspend the contract for a trial period or to form a pilot group as an experiment.

In order to further such a cooperative labor-management relationship, the company recognizes that management must routinely share business information with the union, that it must solicit union views and ideas regarding opportunities for improvement, and that it must acknowledge the union's contribution to organizational accomplishments. In turn, the union must be interested in exploring different ways of carrying out the labor-management relationship, become reasonably knowledgeable about productivity and QWL issues in the operation, not be overly protective of its role in communicating with workers, and be dependable in implementing agreed-on actions. This program represents an entirely new approach to labor-management relations as it seeks to move them to a new cooperative stance.

Labor and management still disagree and will continue to disagree on many issues, but they also have come to recognize that their mutual interests basically outweigh their differences. American unions always have been job conscious and want to protect their members' jobs, and today most of them realize that they can do so best by working with, not against, employers. Thus labor and management are working together more cooperatively to strengthen the efficiency of American industry.

12
Implications for the Future

Conclusions from the Study

Manufacturing companies across a broad array of industries are introducing computer-based technologies in an effort to strengthen and reassert their competitive positions in product markets. Their employees and unions are aware of the need for advanced technology. Thus, resistance to change has been minimal, except among lower-level managers who are fearful of its impact on them. To a considerable degree, companies have neglected this group, focusing instead on the production and maintenance work force. Many companies, however, are turning their attention to solving problems within management.

The human resource function is vital in planning for and implementing new technology. In a period of intensified and persistent product market competition, domestic and foreign, companies must foster innovation in both products and technology. In terms of technology, the microelectronic revolution, as symbolized by the chip, has opened entirely new ways of manufacturing products. Such computer-based technologies serve to increase productivity, reduce production costs, improve product reliability, and, most important, provide greater flexibility with which to respond to product market changes.

Management has discretion about how it fits the new technology into the workplace. Companies can use new technology in ways designed to minimize worker input and deemphasize worker skill or in ways that give greater scope to worker input and broaden worker skill. Companies that have given greatest recognition to the importance of the human input into the production process have achieved the best results with new technology.

That recognition begins with giving employees a voice in the planning and implementation of new technology. Employees have worthwhile ideas to contribute that can help to prevent problems later in the operational stage and generally facilitate the debugging process. Although only a minority of companies have involved the production work force in the design planning for new technology, some indicated that they would do so in the future, and almost all of them involve the work force in the implementation stage.

Beyond the planning for new technology, there is a growing recognition that the human input into the production process is as important as the technology being utilized. Thus companies are reorganizing their approaches to work. Many are training workers to be more broadly skilled and to have greater autonomy in performing their jobs. Most employees are desirous of participating in decision making with respect to their work, and companies have used introduction of new technology as an occasion also to introduce, or expand, programs of employee participation.

Not all the human effects of advanced technology are necessarily positive. Even when employees have enjoyed employment security, new technology has not been costless to all of them. While many have benefited through upgrading, expanded jobs, and more interesting work, some have been transferred to other jobs no better, and possibly worse, than their former ones. Any kind of transfer, moreover, means a loss of familiar surroundings, membership in a work group, and sometimes status and power. The one instance of attempted sabotage of new technology we encountered was perpetrated by employees displaced by that technology and transferred to comparable-paying jobs elsewhere in the plant.

New technology also can pose a threat to job security. Although the aim of introducing programmable automation is to increase competitiveness, the resulting productivity is sometimes greater than the growth in product sales, necessitating employment cutbacks. Certainly most of the companies studied have suffered reductions in employment during the past decade, generally because of recession and product market loss. New technology often allowed lost market shares to be recouped and consequently the lost employment to be at least partially restored. In a few cases, increased competitiveness even led to greater employment. Thus advanced manufacturing technology need not have a deleterious effect on employment and, depending on particular product market conditions, may even contribute to an expansion of the number of jobs, as other studies have found.[1]

The layoff of workers as a result of new technology need not occur, even in the face of employment decline. In order to minimize adverse effects on employees, many companies try to follow a strategy of introducing new technology during the upward phase of the business cycle. Even in the absence of a planned strategy, such timing tends to occur because companies invest more heavily in new plant and equipment during economic expansions. Thus the normal operation of the investment cycle itself tends to minimize adverse employment effects of new technology.

Beyond this, companies can take specific actions to prevent innovation from leading to layoffs. The fact that new technology is customarily introduced gradually provides time to mesh human resource planning with strategic planning for the introduction of new products and processes. The jobs that will be growing or declining in number and the new ones that will be created must be identified; the qualifications for new or altered jobs must be determined.

Good human resource planning permits management to maximize the use of normal attrition—voluntary quits, retirements, and deaths—to trim the work force, when necessary, before new technology is introduced. Using attrition to prevent layoffs, however, often requires other specific activities to avoid adding employees in the planning phase only to have to let them go when the technology is actually implemented. Techniques for preventing this include holding down hiring of new permanent employees and using instead overtime, temporary workers, or contracting out. Attrition also can be speeded up by offers of special early retirement.

Effecting transfers in order to prevent loss of employment is another principal element in human resources planning. Smoothly effecting transfers depends on astute human resource management because almost all facets of employee relations are involved—recruitment, training, transfer rights, and seniority practices. A formidable barrier to the transfer of displaced employees can be their lack of qualifications for other available jobs, but this problem may be overcome by training them in new skills.

Training is the key to successful implementation of computer-based technology. It must be conducted at all levels, from top management to production workers, for everyone's work is affected. Given the fact that implementing CIM is a continuous process, training also must be conducted on an ongoing basis, in line with continuing advances in programmable automation.

Companies that do not adequately retrain employees run into problems in effectively utilizing advanced technology. To ensure that training and retraining will be successful, companies must carefully assess the new types of skills demanded, build training costs into project budgets, capitalize those costs over time as the equipment is, and be sure that the training can be replicated.

As companies move further along the road to involving employees in decision making, they cannot neglect human relations training. A typical bureaucratic organization with an authoritarian style of management cannot create employee involvement overnight; time, effort, and resources are needed to change a culture. Of primary importance are a substantial commitment to change and a recognition that giving production workers decision-making authority upsets the existing power structure of a plant. Top management must be prepared to deal with the consequences of these changes. People must be taught how to interact in group situations without antagonizing one another. Managerial personnel, who must become group leaders rather than production pushers, are particularly in need of human relations training.

For unionized facilities, the new technology has significant labor relations implications. Planning that anticipates problems in this area is essential. The first step is identification of the possible areas of conflict: transfer rights, assignment of jobs to the bargaining unit, flexibility in work force utilization, wage rates for new or altered jobs, assignment of individuals to new jobs, work schedules, incentive systems, rights of displaced employees, and job and income security. The next step is planning means of resolving conflict, whether special joint labor-management committees or regular collective bargaining procedures.

Unions do not resist advanced manufacturing methods. An effective communications program will avoid the building up of resistance by convincing union leaders and members that computer-based technology is necessary to make a facility competitive and thus enable it to provide jobs for the bulk of its present work force. The communications program must give advance notice of impending change, including information on its nature, the date of its inauguration, the effects it will have on the employees, and the ways in which the company plans to aid those who might be adversely affected by it.

Changes in seniority structures, job classification systems, and compensation schemes may become necessary to exploit new technology, and disputes inevitably arise when management seeks to secure collective bargaining agreement modifications. Even in these areas, however, progress has been made, particularly with respect to reducing the number of separate job classifications. The collective bargaining process has proved capable in the past of resolving workplace conflicts, and it is proving so today with respect to technological innovation.

In fact, the introduction of major technological change can also present management with an opportunity to try to change the labor-management climate from an adversarial to a more cooperative relationship. To that end, unions should be invited to participate in the implementation, and even the planning, of the change. If a more harmonious atmosphere is to develop, however, management must be sincere and open with the union, avoiding threats or actions that undercut the union's position. There is no guarantee that all local unions will respond positively, but most will, making it worth management's efforts to attempt to forge a better relationship.

If the transition to computer-based manufacturing is to be accomplished smoothly, management must plan carefully and should involve the employee relations function from the beginning of that planning. A second imperative is communication—why change is needed, what it will be, when it is coming, how it will affect employees, and what programs are being formulated to ease that impact. Since computer-based technology eliminates some jobs, creates new ones, and changes the requirements of others, training of employees at all levels is essential. Companies are learning that good human input is essential to the operation of advanced sophisticated systems. Given the importance of people in keeping computer-based technology operating efficiently, companies are paying special attention to the achievement of greater employee involvement.

Living with Technological Change

Advanced computer-based manufacturing has implications for the entire society as well as for the companies, unions, and employees directly involved in it. America's manufacturing base is imperiled. Unless industry can move quickly and efficiently toward CIM, further erosion could occur. Thus society must learn to live with technological change as a continual process.

Public policy should encourage the development and implementation of advanced manufacturing methods, preferably through tax policies that foster increased capital investment. The federal government should continue and expand its support of basic and applied research in technology and science, including behavioral science.

The fear of so-called technological unemployment should not deter society from fostering new production methods; the failure to adopt advanced technology can have an even more devastating effect on employment. Although programmable automation is altering the types of jobs available, just as technological innovation has been significantly changing the structure of the work force since the industrial revolution began, the shifts are for the most part gradual.

Public policy should not be directed at discouraging innovation but at aiding those who may be adversely affected by it. The recent mandating of the continuation of health insurance for laid-off workers is an example of such a policy. Placing the entire burden on industry, however, ignores the fact that not all companies are equally able to shoulder that burden; thus government must assume some responsibility for aiding the displaced.

The workerless factory is not imminent. Even the road to CIM will be a long, hard one, with many mistakes along the way, but companies will learn from those errors. Manufacturing is becoming more efficient, as revealed by a resurgence in its rate of productivity growth. Other sectors of the economy, however, lag far behind manufacturing with respect to productivity improvement. Thus manufacturing cannot be looked to as a major source of employment growth, so there will be more interindustry shifts in employment.

For new technology to have untoward impact on employment, the nation would have to see its productivity—output per man-hour—rise at an astronomical rate. In recent years, productivity growth has been very low. Some observers see a resurgence in the rate of national productivity growth, but the most optimistic of them project an annual rate of about 1.5 percent. Such an annual increase of under 2 percent would contribute to economic growth and thus need not have a negative impact on employment. From the end of World War II until the mid-1960s, the United States enjoyed a 2.5 to 3 percent annual productivity growth rate, yet it expanded the number of jobs by some 20 million and experienced low rates of unemployment. With the labor force expanding much more slowly in the coming decade, the United States should be able to increase productivity, expand jobs, and reduce unemployment, particularly if that improved productivity helps to make its manufactured products more competitive.

Even if increased productivity does not eliminate jobs faster than attrition trims the work forces of affected industries or the displaced can be retrained for other jobs, what about the new workers coming into the labor market for whom those jobs will no longer exist? First, economic growth should be providing alternative jobs for them in other sectors—21 million new jobs by 2000 (as compared with 1986), according to the Bureau of Labor Statistics' (BLS) moderate economic growth projection.[2] Second, there will be fewer new workers, and that will mitigate any adverse employment effects of technological innovation. In fact, in the 1990s, the nation's labor market problem could well shift from a shortage of jobs to a shortage of workers to fill the jobs that will be available; in New England, this is already the case.

This leaves the question of skills: what happens to the people who do not have the skills to become software and hardware technicians? Where do they fit into this new computerized world? First, the vast number of jobs will not require new skills. According to BLS, by 2000 the number of new jobs as janitors and cleaners (604,000) and truck drivers (505,000) will be two and a half times those as computer systems analysts (251,000) and electrical and electronic engineers (192,000). The growth rate for jobs associated with the computer will be very high, but in absolute numbers it will pale compared with that for more traditional occupations.

Furthermore, to the degree that new skills are needed, people will acquire them. The pattern that may emerge in the future is that young people, instead of taking factory jobs following graduation from high school, will spend two years at a community college learning to become computer hardware or software technicians. In other words, fewer people will become factory operatives, and more people will become information operatives. The notion that there is a huge sector of the population too unintelligent for anything but completely unskilled work has been raised and debunked in every generation, as it is likely to be in the coming generations.

Government has a role in this process: to help provide the education and training needed, particularly by minorities, who will comprise a growing proportion of the labor force. For those still in school, state and local governments will be the ones to shoulder the burden. For those in industry who must be retrained for new and altered jobs, industry itself must bear much of the responsibility. Indeed most respondents to the IRC opinion survey believe that displaced workers can be retrained for other jobs. They say that the primary responsibility for funding such training rests with industry (on average, respondents indicate that 43 percent of the responsibility for funding such retraining rests with industry and only 21 percent with government).

With respect to counseling displaced workers and helping them to find employment elsewhere, the respondents placed 50 percent of the responsibility on industry and only 18 percent on government, and 13 percent on the workers themselves. Interestingly, the British respondents to the survey conducted in the United Kingdom placed less emphasis on industry's role and more on that of government. These differences appear to reflect the different roles government plays in the two countries and the stronger American emphasis on individual responsibility.

Yet respondents acknowledged that government has some responsibility to aid workers in making a transition to alternative employment. This is particularly true for workers in smaller companies, which lack the resources or experience needed to retrain employees. The government effort, however, can be a cooperative one with industry and involve all levels of government—federal, state, and local. A number of states do run training programs, sometimes in concert with industry, and these have been most helpful in preparing workers for higher-level jobs associated with computer-based technology. Other states should follow their lead.

The major contribution of the federal government to the transition to advanced manufacturing technology is ensuring the economic growth that underlies high levels of employment in a society. An economy must grow rapidly enough to generate new jobs to accommodate both an enlarged labor force and the displacement resulting from productivity improvement. From now until the year 2000, a 2.4 percent rate of growth as assumed in the BLS moderate projection would accomplish that objective. Such a rate of growth is in line with what the United States has experienced in the last few years. Should gross national product increase at a 3.0 percent rate, BLS sees unemployment dropping to 4.5 percent by 2000.

Change and adaptation to change have been the pattern that has characterized the entire history of the industrial revolution. Each new innovation, from Arkwright's flying shuttle in the late eighteenth-century textile industry to programmable automation in the late twentieth century, eliminated some jobs, causing a painful transition for some workers and regions. Economic growth, however, to which the technological progress contributed, led to the creation of more jobs than previously existed. To assume that the pattern will be otherwise now is to fly in the face of historic experience. Until such time as all citizens have enough goods and services, public as well as private, to satisfy their wants, there is plenty of room for further growth, and workers will be required to produce the goods and services.

Cushioning the Impact of Change

Although technological change cannot be held responsible for higher levels of unemployment in the country, it can cause distress for particular workers. When displacement occurs, workers who have become highly specialized in specific skills that are no longer needed, older workers, and workers with poor educational backgrounds find it difficult to locate new jobs, and when they do, their wage rates usually are far below what they had earned before. Unfortunately, such labor force disruption is a price that a society must pay for economic progress.

This does not mean that the individuals who are harmed by new technology must bear the entire cost while the rest of society reaps the benefits. There is both human and economic justification for special efforts to ameliorate the burden falling on these workers. On humanitarian grounds, undue suffering should be prevented. On economic grounds, providing displaced workers with some income helps to maintain consumer purchasing power, and retraining or relocating them enables them to contribute to national production.

Private and public programs to aid the victims of innovation will have to be fashioned. As important as companies' private efforts will be, governmental programs also will be necessary. Not all companies will be in a position to provide alternative jobs, and the smaller ones will hardly be able to match the larger ones in their ability to retrain displaced workers. The local communities most heavily affected are unlikely to be financially able to carry the burden, nor should they be expected to do so. Structural changes in the economy are extralocal in character. Just as the individual workers who are adversely affected should not have to bear the whole cost of innovation, neither should the communities in which those workers reside. Since the entire society enjoys the benefits of technological advances, it also should share in paying the costs.

The federal government, thus, will have to help ease the transition to new methods of manufacturing. Federal programs of retraining and relocation were in existence in the 1960s and may be required again. Pat Choate, senior policy analyst, TRW Inc., who has called for a national training effort, favors establishing individual training accounts (ITA), whereby displaced workers receive funds to undertake retraining and relocation, where necessary.[3] Legislation favoring this "GI Bill" approach has been introduced in Congress.

The federal government also could help to ease the transition by studying the changes in jobs and providing information on new skill requirements to guide curriculum development in schools and colleges, as well as in private and public training programs. Income maintenance programs may be called for, especially if some areas are badly affected by the combination of the decline of old industries and the advent of new technology.

The educational community has a vital role to play in the transition to advanced technology. Many companies have concluded that a university nearby is an essential element in plant location. Industry-university cooperation in research is growing extremely rapidly, but there is also need for greater cooperation with respect to education and training. Curriculum changes are in order. Engineers must understand the human and organizational implications and interactions of new technology, and those being trained as managers must have greater technical literacy. The latter is extremely important for many observers blame concentration on short-run profit, a greater concern for the company's stock price than its products and technology, and present accounting methods for the tardiness of American industry in adopting advanced manufacturing systems.

Industry-university cooperation in education and training should be expanded. Companies whose engineers are not up to date on computerization should be able to turn to universities to remedy the problem. Universities can help introduce managers to new organizational theories and methods. In fact, cooperation in education and training can be extended to all levels of the labor force, from top managers to plant floor workers. While the company provides the specific training, the university can offer the broader education needed for new technology.

Marching into the Future

U.S. manufacturing has gone through a difficult period since the mid-1970s. The United States emerged from World War II as the dominant economic power. The first postwar decade was a period of great economic achievement. Reconversion from war to peacetime production was easily accomplished, and in response to the pentup demand for goods, manufacturing production surged. With Europe and Japan prostrate, there was no foreign competition; on the contrary, they provided markets for American goods. Productivity grew at a fairly rapid rate and the standard of living rose.

The manufacturing system of mass production thrived, and the bureaucratic structure of corporations seemed to be the best organizational approach. Although new organizational theories were spawned by American behavioral scientists, few American companies implemented them. Many of these American ideas were later applied in the so-called Japanese management approach, but in the 1950s they were largely ignored in the United States. The business attitude could best be described by the popular saying, "If it ain't broke, don't fix it." In this favorable economic environment, a new labor-management relationship evolved. The economic pie was expanding, and American industry was willing to share the gains with labor. Wages rose annually, and an elaborate panoply of fringe benefits—retirement, medical, unemployment—became commonplace.

But the world changes. Europe and Japan were rebuilt, and Third World nations were also developing and entering the arena of manufacturing. A global economy emerged, replacing the old national one. By the 1970s, a combination of high compensation and lagging productivity made the United States a high-cost producer that was careless about product quality. It also fell behind in implementing new technology. Factors beyond industry's control, such as the surge in the value of the U.S. dollar in the 1980s, added to the difficulties. The result was a loss of markets for American goods at home and abroad.

In the past few years, however, American manufacturing has attempted a comeback. It has been introducing computer-based technology and experimenting with new approaches to organization and work. These innovations have begun to bear fruit, for in the past five years, output per manhour in manufacturing has risen at an annual average rate of more than 4 percent. Thus, the gap is closing in rates of productivity growth between the United States and other advanced industrial nations and, in 1986, for the first time since 1950, productivity in American manufacturing outpaced that of competitors. Compensation in the United States, moreover, rose only moderately and less than in nine major industrial nations; indeed, the United States enjoyed a 0.6 percent drop in manufacturing labor costs, while all competitors had increases. With the cheaper dollar, the United States should be poised for further progress in restoring competitiveness.

At the same time, a revolution in the organization of industrial enterprises has been taking place. Layers of management are being stripped away, and the resulting flatter organization reduces the time for communications to move up and down the scalar chain and ensures greater reliability in the interpretation of those messages. Also, decision making is being pushed down the organizational hierarchy, and work is being redesigned to be more meaningful. American manufacturing has begun to move away from the mechanistic structure of the bureaucratic organization, which was compatible with a situation of stable markets and stable technology, to a more open system and organic structure, which permits greater flexibility and easier adaptation to a world of rapidly changing markets and technology.

American manufacturing must guard against a resurgence of complacency and a return to old ways as the situation improves. To the contrary, it must continue to pursue the introduction of advanced manufacturing methods, a more organic management style, employee involvement and new ways of work design, and less adversarial labor-management relations. Global competition is not a passing fad, and the new approaches cannot be treated as such.

U.S. manufacturing can continue its comeback. The human resource and employee relations impacts of computer-based technologies show that no untoward problems have arisen. Employees, and where they are organized, their unions, have been realistic and recognized the need for the new technology, and even for changes in organization and work rules. A major factor in that acceptance has been management's openness and actions designed to ameliorate adverse affects on employees. Thus, if they are to continue down the road to greater competitiveness, companies must adhere to such policies.

A smooth transition to new technology is furthered through advance planning, which includes human resource planning. Companies are learning that the operation of advanced sophisticated systems more than ever requires good human input. To this end, they must carefully assess the skill requirements emerging from new technology, communicate with employees, train them for the new jobs, reorganize work, and include employees in decision making with respect to their work.

Computer-based technology, thus, presents new opportunities, not only to improve manufacturing competitiveness, but also to instill new dignity and excitement into industrial work. The image of factory work invoked by Charlie Chaplin in his famous film *Modern Times,* of a person tightening bolts on an assembly line continuously eight hours a day, five days a week, fifty weeks a year, will become a historic curiosity.

In the computerized future, jobs will encompass broader tasks, with multiskilled workers having greater discretion in their performance and role in decision making. People will be members of work teams, cooperating with other groups, continually learning, and rewarded for their expanded knowledge. Although there will be relatively fewer workers in manufacturing, they may be much more satisfied workers, who can exercise autonomy and intellectual as well as manual skills on the job. Sharp distinctions between workers and managers will be blurred, and all participants in an enterprise will learn to work together to achieve its objectives as well as their own.

This vision of the future will become reality if leading companies continue in the directions they have been experimenting with in this period of adversity and do not return to the status quo ante as the competitive situation improves. If they pursue the new course, the combination of computer-based technology and new approaches to work and organization will bring success to American manufacturing. At the same time, manufacturing could become a model for other sectors of the U.S. economy also undergoing significant technological change involving computers.

The new technology promises a future of improved competitiveness for American industry and, consequently, higher living standards for the population as a whole, but there is also the possibility of increased displacement of workers. The problem for management, and indeed, for society in general, is to determine how to reap the benefits of computer-based technology while minimizing its disruptions. If the transition to CIM is to be accomplished smoothly, management must plan carefully and be prepared to alter organizational structures and methods of management in comformity with the demands of the new technology. Management also must devise programs to ease the impact of change on employees. Companies that do not plan adequately will jeopardize the benefits of CIM. Those that plan well will make a successful transition to this new industrial revolution.

Appendix A: Robotics Study Sponsoring Companies

Amoco Foundation, Inc. (Standard Oil Company of Indiana)
Baltimore Gas and Electric Company
Control Data Corporation
E. I. du Pont de Nemours and Company
Eastman Kodak Company
Exxon Corporation
General Electric Company
The Goodyear Tire & Rubber Company
Hewlett Packard Company
International Business Machines Corporation
Northern Telecom Limited
Northrop Corporation
The Standard Oil Company (Ohio)
Tenneco Inc.
TRW Inc.
United States Steel Corporation
Xerox Corporation

Appendix B: IRC Survey Questionnaire and Responses

Appendix B: *IRC Survey Questionnaire and Responses* • 141

IRC Study of the Impact of Robotics on Human Resources and Employee Relations

This survey was conducted in the U.S. during the period of September 1984 through May 1985 The purpose of the survey was to elicit opinions concerning the effect of robotics on human resources and employee relations activities in manufacturing industries.

The total survey response population was 168. The number of responses to each question is posted in parentheses; the percentages indicated are based on that number.

I. ROBOTICS INTRODUCTION

> For the purpose of the IRC study, "robotics" will be defined broadly to include robots and other programmable automation that make possible computer-integrated flexible manufacturing.

1.
  A. Using the above definition of robotics as a working definition for this study, indicate when you see the major thrust of change occurring.

  (144) a. by 1990 (near future)   60.4% Yes; 29.2% No; 10.4% Can't tell.

  (117) b. by 2000 (far future)   82.1% Yes; 2.6% No; 15.4% Can't tell.

  B. Do you see its widespread usage in manufacturing coming suddenly or gradually?

  (167)   91.6% Gradually; 8.4% Suddenly.

Copyright© 1985, Industrial Relations Counselors, Inc.
All rights reserved.

142 • Computerized Manufacturing and Human Resources

2. Which industries will be key users of robotics, as defined and by when would you expect this to occur? Please check appropriate boxes.

			Now to 1990 (1)	1991 to 2000 (2)
(96)	a.	Primary metal industries	41.7%	58.3%
(145)	b.	Fabricated metal products	69.0	31.0
(136)	c.	Machinery, except electrical	55.9	44.1
(145)	d.	Electric and electronic equipment	75.9	24.1
(152)	e.	Transportation equipment (e.g., motor vehicles and equipment, aircraft and parts, guided missiles, space vehicles, parts)	80.9	19.1
(119)	f.	Instruments and related parts	42.9	57.1
(88)	g.	Food and kindred products	33.0	67.0
(87)	h.	Textile mill products	36.8	63.2
(77)	i.	Paper and allied products	40.3	59.7
(94)	j.	Chemicals and allied products	51.1	48.9
(86)	k.	Petroleum and coal products	29.1	70.9
(97)	l.	Rubber and miscellaneous plastics products	54.6	45.4
(65)	m.	Other manufacturing	29.2	70.8

3. Indicate which of the following are most likely to be significant users of robotics and by when.

			By 1990	After 1990
(162)	a.	Large-sized companies (more than 10,000 employees)	83.3	16.7
(154)	b.	Medium-sized companies (1,000 to 10,000 employees)	32.5	67.5
(120)	c.	Small-sized companies (less than 1,000 employees)	7.5	92.5

Appendix B: IRC Survey Questionnaire and Responses • 143

(164) **4. To what extent do you agree with the following statement?**

> Intelligent introduction of robots to the manufacturing scene makes it imperative that employers take employees into their confidence at every stage.
> *Phillip Lynch, 1982.*

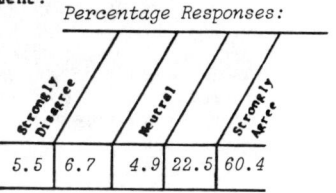

Percentage Responses:

Strongly Disagree		Neutral		Strongly Agree
5.5	6.7	4.9	22.5	60.4

(149) **5. Please RANK the following factors from "1" to "3" in order of their importance to the successful introduction of robotics in existing facilities.**

("1" is the MOST important, and "3" is the LEAST important.)

    _3†_ Labor union cooperation (where employees are organized)

    _1_ Employee understanding and acceptance

    _2_ Employee involvement in planning for introduction

> †*These rankings are based on the highest percentage of respondents specifying such rank for each factor.*

6. Japan is described as the leading user of robotics; what are the major differences between Japan and the United States that should be considered for the effective implementation of robotics here? *(128)*

Rank	Frequency of Response	Item
1	44.5%	Employee involvement and participation: i.e., communication of change to the labor force; attitude that robots are good for the company; lower wages and benefits; profit-sharing bonuses; long-term economic rewards from work; and employee identification with the company/company paternalism.
2	36.7	Job security; lifetime employment.
3	21.9	Cost justification of investment in robotics: i.e., ROI is better because automation is done on a small scale, hence not prohibitively expensive; lower interest rates/easier capitalization.
4	21.1	Nonadversarial union-management relations.
4	21.1	Cultural differences.
6	20.3	Government-business partnership in planning and implementation of new technology.
7	18.0	Long-term investment focus; long-range planning.
8	14.1	Greater coordination between engineering and manufacuturing: i.e, availability of engineering personnel; close relationship between engineering and manufacturing; robotics integrated into the total process and not merely a replacement for people; simpler approach to problem solving.
9	11.7	Manpower shortage.
10	10.9	Training and reeducation.
11	10.2	Dedication to quality.
12	8.6	Responsiveness to the marketplace, including focus on international competition/national industry policy; willingness to change product design, production organization, and greater flexibility in the areas of employee mobility and benefits.

II. REACTIONS TO THE INTRODUCTION OF ROBOTICS

7. Indicate which of the following attitudes towards the introduction of robotics are typically attributable to managers and supervisors.

		Top-level managers			Middle managers			First-level supervisors		
		Number	Yes	No	Number	Yes	No	Number	Yes	No
a.	Awareness of need to robotize	(149)	89.3%	10.7%	(138)	76.1%	23.9%	(132)	40.2%	59.8%
b.	Supportiveness of robotization	(139)	92.1	7.9	(125)	56.8	43.2	(128)	31.3	68.7
c.	Recognition of skill obsolescence issues	(135)	65.2	34.8	(128)	75.8	24.2	(132)	65.2	34.8
d.	Willingness to accommodate to change	(138)	83.3	16.7	(128)	51.6	48.4	(122)	26.2	73.8

8. How would you categorize the typical reactions to robotics among managers and supervisors?

Percentage Responses:

			Strongly Negative		Neutral		Strongly Positive
(154)	a.	Top-level managers	0.6	3.2	12.3	44.2	39.6
(154)	b.	Middle managers	1.9	14.9	39.6	36.4	7.1
(151)	c.	First-level supervisors	6.6	48.3	32.5	9.3	3.3

9. To what extent does a company's introduction of robotics in production operations cause anxiety among:

Percentage Responses:

			To a Great Extent		To Some Extent		Not at All
(163)	a.	Production workers	52.8	28.2	15.3	2.5	1.2
(160)	b.	Technical workers	10.6	15.0	32.5	28.1	13.8
(160)	c.	First-line supervisors	21.3	30.6	42.5	5.0	0.6
(159)	d.	Middle management	5.7	17.0	41.5	27.0	8.8
(160)	e.	Top management	1.3	2.5	20.6	36.3	39.4

10.

A. If you were a 45 year-old worker in a factory where robotics was to be introduced, to what extent do you believe the following areas would be of concern to you?

Percentage Responses:

		Very Much		Some		Not at All
(161)	a. Job security	77.0	11.2	8.7	3.1	0.0
(159)	b. Closer monitoring of job performance	22.6	23.9	39.0	10.1	4.4
(159)	c. Continuous demands for new technical knowledge	33.3	31.5	30.2	3.1	1.9
(162)	d. Need to change to a different job	35.2	38.3	18.5	6.8	1.2
(153)	e. Social interaction with co-workers	11.1	18.3	28.1	27.5	15.0

B. If you were a 25 year-old worker in a factory where robotics was to be introduced, to what extent do you believe the following areas would be of concern to you?

Percentage Responses:

		Very Much		Some		Not at All
(162)	a. Job security	35.8	16.0	35.2	9.9	3.1
(158)	b. Closer monitoring of job performance	19.0	20.2	39.2	16.5	5.1
(160)	c. Continuous demands for new technical knowledge	18.1	18.1	34.4	18.8	10.6
(161)	d. Need to change to a different job	10.6	18.0	32.9	28.6	9.9
(152)	e. Social interaction with co-workers	6.6	12.5	35.5	25.0	20.4

11. Listed below are actions or strategies that unions might take in relation to the introduction of robotics. Please RANK them from "1" to "8" in order of the priority you believe union leaders will give them.
("1" is the MOST emphasis, and "8" is the LEAST emphasis.)

(155) **Union Leaders** ▶ *Rank based on average response.*

2	Require retraining of displaced workers
4	Seek to influence how robotics is introduced
8	Seek decision power on broad management issues
1	Enhance job security for members
5	Try to include jobs related to robotics in bargaining unit
6	Seek compensation upgrading as an incentive
7	Accept introduction as a means to protect jobs in the plant
3	Seek job protections for a limited time period

12. In terms of your personal reactions, to what extent do you agree with the following statement?

(168)

Percentage Responses:

The robot question has been overplayed a little bit. After all, it's nothing but another form of automation. *Donald Ephlin, 1982.*	Strongly Disagree		Neutral		Strongly Agree
	13.1	19.0	11.3	29.8	26.8

III. IMPACT OF ROBOTICS

13. The following is a list of some major results ascribed to the use of robotics. To what extent do you think these results will be realized in manufacturing by 1990?

Percentage Responses:

			Not at All		To Some Extent		To a Great Extent
(163)	a.	Reduced labor content in production process	0.0	4.9	43.0	29.4	22.7
(162)	b.	Reduced production labor costs	0.0	9.3	37.6	31.5	21.6
(163)	c.	Reduced overall production costs	3.7	13.5	35.0	30.1	17.8
(160)	d.	Workers freed from repetitive jobs	6.9	14.4	28.1	27.5	23.1
(162)	e.	Workers freed from dangerous jobs	2.5	9.2	22.2	27.2	38.9
(158)	f.	Flexibility in changing outputs of manufacturing processes	4.4	12.0	24.1	35.4	24.1
(162)	g.	Increased management control of the work process	1.9	11.7	30.8	35.8	19.8
(154)	h.	Jobs removed from bargaining unit	5.8	22.1	45.5	18.8	7.8
(162)	i.	Improved quality of products	0.6	7.4	20.4	38.3	33.3
(157)	j.	Improved response to the marketplace	7.0	18.5	28.0	27.4	19.1

14. To what extent do you agree with the following statements?

Percentage Responses:

(161) a. As robots become tools of automated factory systems, erosion of union strength could result.
Free Labor World, 05/81.

Strongly Disagree		Neutral		Strongly Agree
3.1	10.6	22.4	47.8	16.1

(162) b. Robots may encroach on jobs traditionally held by minorities and women.
Leap & Pizzolatto, 1983.

Percentage Responses:

9.3	13.5	17.3	42.6	17.3

(156) c. As the economy robotizes and domestic jobs are lost to foreign production, 10 million to 15 million manufacturing workers and a similar number of service workers likely will be displaced from their existing jobs. Much of this displacement will occur in the mid- to late 1980s.
Pat Choate, 1982.

Percentage Responses:

34.6	29.5	10.9	19.2	5.8

148 • *Computerized Manufacturing and Human Resources*

15. What do you think will happen to employment as a result of robotics?

    a. Directly (in the U.S. manufacturing industries)

Percentage Responses:

	Large Reduction		No Effect		Large Increase
(166) In 1990 compared to 1984	1.8	46.4	41.6	9.0	1.2
(167) In 2000 compared to 1984	22.8	41.9	14.3	13.8	7.2

   b. Indirectly (in the overall U.S. economy)

(158) In 1990 compared to 1984	0.6	16.5	58.2	22.8	1.9
(158) In 2000 compared to 1984	3.2	26.6	25.3	33.5	11.4

16. What do you think is the likelihood of a displaced worker . . .

Percentage Responses:

	Highly Unlikely		Neutral		Highly Likely
(164) a. finding a new job in the same field	15.2	54.9	17.7	9.2	3.0
(164) b. training for a new field	0.6	14.6	26.9	45.1	12.8
(162) c. transferring to a new field	1.9	4.9	28.4	53.7	11.1
(163) d. getting a higher paying job	23.3	36.8	27.0	11.1	1.8
(163) e. getting a lower paying job	0.6	12.9	25.2	41.7	19.6
(163) f. experiencing long-term unemployment	5.5	19.0	25.8	38.7	11.0
(163) g. needing to relocate	0.6	8.6	19.6	57.1	14.1

Appendix B: IRC Survey Questionnaire and Responses • 149

> The most remarkable thing about the job-displacement and the job-creation impacts of industrial robots is the skill twist.... The jobs eliminated are semiskilled or unskilled, while the jobs created require significant technical background.
>
> H. Allan Hunt and Timothy L. Hunt, 1983.

17. What is the likelihood that this "skill twist" will add significantly to the pool of U.S. workers unable to qualify for any available jobs?

Percentage Responses:

		Highly Unlikely		Neutral		Highly Likely
(164)	a. Near future (by 1990)	12.8	16.5	29.8	34.8	6.1
(162)	b. Far future (by 2000)	8.6	19.2	22.2	31.5	18.5

18. Indicate to what extent you believe robotics will significantly change each of the following work factors for U.S. workers?

Percentage Responses:

		Significant Decrease		No Change		Significant Increase
(159)	a. Work pressure	1.3	15.1	47.2	28.9	7.5
(157)	b. Work autonomy	11.5	30.5	21.0	32.5	4.5
(159)	c. Control of work process	13.2	28.9	13.2	33.4	11.3
(156)	d. Work schedule/shift work	2.6	15.3	48.1	24.4	9.6
(158)	e. Task variety	5.1	19.0	18.4	45.6	12.0
(162)	f. Physical effort	28.4	59.9	10.5	1.2	0.0
(158)	g. Skill requirements	3.2	7.0	2.5	54.4	32.9
(140)	h. Work sharing	3.6	4.3	49.2	32.9	10.0

> In our traditional job system, most workers receive rewards based on the effort they expend. Computer-integrated manufacturing technology unhinges those relationships because machine productivity ultimately is unrelated to the activity of the workers.
>
> Sara Kiesler, Carnegie-Mellon University, 1983

19. Given the breaking of the linkage between output and worker effort, what will happen to the present incentive systems of compensation for production workers?

Percentage Responses: Disappear / / / / Expand (No Change middle)

(148)   16.9 | 38.5 | 25.0 | 14.2 | 5.4

20A. Indicate to what extent you believe the use of robotics will affect the role of each of the following company employee relations activities?

	Item	SER		NC		SDR†
(162)	a. Manpower planning	9.3%	35.1%	32.1%	19.8%	3.7%
(162)	b. Recruitment and selection	13.6	51.2	29.0	5.0	1.2
(165)	c. Training and development	42.4	47.8	4.3	4.3	1.2
(160)	d. Occupational safety and health	8.8	23.7	37.5	27.5	2.5
(162)	e. Employee participation programs	17.3	46.9	27.2	7.4	1.2
(164)	f. Labor relations	10.4	29.9	39.0	18.3	2.4
(159)	g. University/external relations	18.9	45.9	32.7	2.5	0.0
(162)	h. Compensation	1.9	34.6	54.3	8.0	1.2
(160)	i. Fringe benefits	1.9	21.9	66.8	7.5	1.9
(6)	j. Other specific responses:					
	Communications	16.7				
	Performance/Motivation		16.7			
	Management and Organizational Development	16.7				
	Collective Bargaining	16.7				
	Education	16.7				
	EEO		16.7			

†Significantly Expand Role; Expand; No Change; Diminish; Significantly Diminish.

20B. Of the activities listed above, please select the <u>one</u> that you think will be most affected by robotics.

(155)

Rank	Frequency of Response	Item
1	56.1%	Training and development
2	12.3	Employee participation programs
3	9.7	Labor relations
4	6.5	Recruitment and selection
5	5.2	Manpower planning
6	3.2	Occupational safety and health
7	2.6	University/external relations
8	0.6	Compensation
	0.6	Benefits
	0.6	Communications
	0.6	Performance/motivation
	0.6	Organizational development

20C. Please comment on how the activity you have selected will change.
(124)
Training and development
    21.0%   Intensification of training activity by companies
    18.5   More technical, higher skills development; more general knowledge/multifunctional
    10.5   Effective retraining coordinated with skill requirements
    6.5   Retraining displaced workers
    0.8   Off-site training
    0.8   Training for support, maintenance

Employee participation programs
    6.5%   Need for more of this activity to make the introduction successful
    4.0   Work force will contribute to running business in a meaningful way
    1.6   Greater dependence on employees to act independently
    1.6   Workers will seek greater control over work environment
    1.6   Reduced employment will diminish the need for participation programs

Labor relations
    3.2%   Labor union resistance
    2.4   Closer cooperation between unions and management
    1.6   Establishment of policies for displaced workers
    0.8   Increased management control over labor

Recruitment and selection
    4.0%   More emphasis placed on carefully matching skills to technically complex jobs
    1.6   Methods will be changed to attract skilled people in high demand

Manpower planning
    3.2%   More planning done to take into account "skill twist"

Occupational safety and health
    1.6%   Robots will take the dangerous and monotonous jobs

University/external relations
    2.4%   Greater linkages between business and academia promoted so that business needs can influence skills development

Compensation
    0.8%   Development of new systems that reward robotics utilization and maintenance

Communications
    0.8%   Need for advance discussion with all employees

Performance/motivation
    0.8%   Development of new system for performance measurement and reward

IV. FUTURE ISSUES

21. Overall, how important is the wider use of robotics to the competitive position of the United States in the world economy?

(163)

Not at All Important		Somewhat Important		Very Important
0.0	1.8	11.7	19.0	67.5

Percentage Responses:

22. Historically, management planning has been predicated on short-term, primarily financial performance considerations. Will robotics cause a change in the investment planning of industrial leaders:

(153) a. By forcing them to take a longer term view of their investment decisions? 75.2% Yes; 24.8% No.

(146) b. By forcing them to consider the human resources impact of the investment decision 63.0% Yes; 37.0% No.

23. In the long run, how will robotics affect the following issues?

	Much Less Likely		No Change		Much More Likely
(159) a. Reduction of work time	1.3	6.3	44.0	33.3	15.1
(148) b. Job sharing	0.7	6.7	46.6	33.8	12.2

	Much Less Necessary		No Change		Much More Necessary
(158) c. Career shift	0.0	2.5	7.0	61.4	29.1

	Much Shorter		No Change		Much Longer
(160) d. Length of work life	1.3	26.8	47.5	16.3	8.1

24. Please check to indicate when you think the United States will be able to develop sufficiently skilled personnel in each of the following areas to support the building, operation, and maintenance of robotics.

		Personnel		
		by 1990	by 2000	Number
a.	Hardware design	80.8%	19.2%	(151)
b.	Software design	69.7	30.3	(155)
c.	Manufacturing	71.9	28.1	(153)
d.	Maintenance	68.6	31.4	(153)
e.	Operation	75.8	24.2	(149)
f.	General management	59.5	40.5	(148)

25. Please identify the specific skills that you believe will most be needed for the
(126) growth and application of robotics within the next 10-15 years.

Frequency of Response	Response
47.6%	Software design
37.3	Systems integration planning and applications engineering
31.7	Hardware design
18.3	General and personnel management
16.7	Maintenance
11.1	Computer literacy
9.5	Manufacturing
6.3	Operations
3.2	Financial/Business
2.4	Interpersonal skills
1.6	Ergonomics
0.8	All skills listed in question 24 above
0.8	Product design

26.
   A. Is the educational system in the United States currently geared to produce sufficiently skilled personnel?

   (163)   23.9% Yes; 60.1 No; 16.0 Can't tell.

   B. How should the responsibility to retrain displaced workers be distributed?
      Please distribute 100 percent among the following:

   (168) 1. With respect to the funding of retraining:

   20.9% Government   (Percentage distribution based on average response.)
   43.4 Industry
   7.1 Labor unions
   13.8 Educational systems
   1.7 Voluntary groups
   13.1 Workers

   Please distribute 100 percent among the following:

   (168) 2. With respect to the conduct of retraining:

   11.2% Government
   41.2 Industry
   8.8 Labor unions
   31.4 Educational systems
   2.1 Voluntary groups
   5.3 Workers

   C. To what extent can displaced workers be redeployed within the company?

   Percentage Responses:

   (157)

Not at All	To Some Extent			To a Great Extent
0.6	8.9	50.3	22.3	17.8

   D. How should the responsibility to handle outplacement for displaced workers be distributed?
      Please distribute 100 percent among the following:

   (168) 18.4% Government
   49.5 Industry
   13.1 Labor unions
   3.4 Educational systems
   2.7 Voluntary groups
   12.9 Workers

27. What effects do you believe the robotics revolution will have on society in the future?

			SD		NC		SI†
(159)	a.	Standards of living	1.9%	9.4%	19.5%	53.5%	15.7%
(156)	b.	Quality of life	1.9	9.0	16.0	57.1	16.0
(155)	c.	Individual freedom	4.5	7.8	42.6	37.4	7.7
(154)	d.	Government involvement in economic decision-making	2.6	11.7	63.6	18.9	3.2
(7)	e.	Other specific responses:					
		Wider income distribution					14.3
		Pressure to become better educated				14.3	14.3
		Privacy	14.3				
		Quality of work				14.3	
		International competition					14.3
		Weakening of unions					14.3

†Significant Decrease; No Change; Significant Increase.

28. Overall, what do you think are the key issues generated by the trend toward introduction of robotics?

   (Percentage based on frequency of response.)

   a. Within the next decade:
   - 39.0% Training/retraining
   - 31.6 Job security, displacement, relocation
   - 24.3 Financial issues: funding, investment, industry survival
   - 19.9 Manufacturing issues: new technology applied to manufacturing, unmanned factories, quality of production
   - 17.6 Employment, recruitment of skilled personnel, educational requirements
   - 14.0 Improved international competitive position, economic growth, change in the economic base
   - 12.5 Business management issues: strategic planning, management ability to adapt to change, greater management control over work processes, changes in organization structure
   - 10.3 Employee participation and acceptance
   - 8.8 Change in traditional worker/management and labor relations
   - 7.4 Change in the nature and definition of work and manpower utilization
   - 6.6 Skill twist
   - 5.9 Compensation
   - 5.9 Wider gap between rich and poor
   - 3.7 Shift to service economy
   - 2.9 Ethical/moral dimension of robotics use, dehumanization of the work place
   - 2.2 Quality of work/life
   - 2.2 Greater safety in working conditions
   - 0.7 Shorter working time, more leisure time

(Continued on page 16.)

b. Beyond:
- 26.7% Manufacturing issues; new technology development, unmanned factories, quality of production
- 24.8 Employment, recruitment of skilled personnel, education requirements
- 20.8 Job security, displacement, relocation
- 17.8 Retraining, training
- 17.8 Improved international competitive position; economic growth; change in the economic base
- 8.9 Financial issues; cost justification, funding, investment, industry survival
- 8.9 Business management issues: strategic planning, management adaptability to change, greater management control over work processes
- 8.9 Shift to service economy
- 8.9 Quality of work/life
- 6.9 Skill twist
- 6.9 Employee participation and acceptance
- 6.9 Wider gap between rich and poor
- 6.9 Ethical/moral dimension of robotics use; dehumanization of the work place
- 5.0 Change in traditional worker/management and labor relations
- 4.0 Shorter working time/more leisure
- 4.0 Change in the nature and definition of work
- 1.0 Compensation

29. To what extent do you believe the following institutions will be affected by robotics?

Percentage Responses:

		Not at All	To Some Extent		To a Great Extent	
(163)	a. Business	0.0	1.8	14.7	38.7	44.8
(162)	b. Government	9.3	14.2	47.5	24.1	4.9
(162)	c. Unions	0.6	3.1	15.4	40.8	40.1
(164)	d. Educational institutions	0.6	11.6	30.5	36.6	20.7
(157)	e. Professional associations	5.1	17.8	39.5	23.6	14.0

30. To what extent do you agree with the following statement concerning the more distant future?

(160)

Percentage Responses:

By 2025, it is conceivable that more sophisticated robots will replace almost all operatives in manufacturing. Robert Ayers and Steve Miller, 1982.	Strongly Agree		Neutral		Strongly Disagree
	13.8	33.7	12.5	28.1	11.9

31. Please give the names and affiliations of three people whom you believe to be the most informed on the subject of robotics.
    (Statistics were not compiled on this information.)

Appendix B: IRC Survey Questionnaire and Responses • 157

(27) 32. Please use the following space to comment on relevant issues concerning the impact of robotics which were not covered in this questionnaire.

Frequency of Response	Response
25.9%	Significant changes to organization structure to adapt to new technology; significant changes in the personnel function, O.D. function; participative management; keeping qualified personnel
25.9	Impact on the world economy, change in the U.S. industry mix, capital formation to convert heavy manufacturing to robotics use, improved U.S. competitiveness driving steady employment, impact of foreign robotics development on U.S. competitive status
18.5	The shake-out of the robot business through start-up businessses, mergers, and bankruptcies; development of robotic technology and data base
18.5	Management of new technology: management ability to plan and effectively use increased productivity, impact of the speed of robotics introduction
18.5	Wealth distribution, redefinition of the work ethic, improved quality of life
3.7	Higher level of education
3.7	Effect on office/service operations
3.7	Minimal people impact as robotics application will occur in only certain operations
3.7	Occupational safety and health aspects
3.7	Industrial sabotage

V. BACKGROUND INFORMATION

(163) 33. What is your level of expertise in the field?
    a. Expert in robotics   17.8%
    b. Knowledgeable about robotics   33.7
    c. Acquainted with robotics   48.5

(162) 34. What is your major field of work?
    a. Economics/Finance   11.7%
    b. Engineering/Computer Sciences   22.2
    c. Labor Relations   16.0
    d. General Management   21.0
    e. Human Resources Management   14.2
    f. Social Sciences   3.1
    g. Physical Sciences   1.9
    h. Other (Please specify)   9.9†
        †Manufacturing   [4.4]
        Research and Development   [1.2]
        Educational Technology   [0.6]
        Science and Industry Policy   [0.6]
        Consulting   [1.2]
        Nonspecified   [1.9]

(164) 35. What is your primary affiliation?
    a. Academia   18.3%
    b. Business   56.7
    c. Government   7.3
    d. Research institute   5.5
    e. Labor union   11.0
    f. Media   0.0
    g. Other (Nonspecified)   1.2

(106) 36. What if any, is your industry affiliation (e.g., textiles)?

14.1%	Diverse manufacturing/conglomerate	5.7%	Electrical
9.4	High tech (computers and peripherals)	5.7	Primary metals/metalworking
		4.7	Transportation equipment
9.4	Petroleum/energy	4.7	Aerospace
8.5	Food products/consumer goods	3.8	Tire and rubber products
7.5	Chemicals and allied products/pharmaceuticals	3.8	Telecommunications
		1.9	Finance
6.6	Robotics	1.9	Services
5.7	Automotive manufacture	6.6	Other

37. If you are in a manufacturing business, to what degree are your company's production workers unionized?

Percentage Responses:

(75)

Not Organized		Moderately Organized		Heavily Organized
18.7	10.6	20.0	20.0	30.7

(93) 38. If you are in a business, please indicate your company size.

Less than 1,000 employees	14.0%
1,000 to 10,000 employeees	17.2
More than 10,000 employees	60.2
Not applicable	8.6

(139) 39. Where are you located?

a.	Northeast	41.7%
b.	Midwest	29.5
c.	South	5.0
d.	West	7.2
e.	Other	16.6†
	†Canada	[0.7]
	Worldwide	[6.5]
	Nationwide	[9.4]

(144) 40. Please indicate your age.

a.	Under 30	4.9%
b.	30-45	47.9
c.	46-55	27.8
d.	56-65	16.6
e.	Over 65	2.8

(143) 41. Please indicate your sex.

| a. | Female | 9.8% |
| b. | Male | 90.2 |

Notes

Foreword and Acknowledgments

1. Richard A. Beaumont and Roy B. Helfgott, *Management, Automation, and People* (New York: Industrial Relations Counselors, 1964).

Introduction

1. See, for example, Robert Nisbet, *History of the Idea of Progress* (New York: Basic Books, 1980).
2. Nathan Rosenberg, *Technology and American Economic Growth* (Armonk, N.Y.: M.E. Sharpe, 1972), esp. chap. 1.
3. See Robert Solow, "Technical Change and the Aggregate Production Function," *Review of Economics and Statistics* (August 1957).
4. See, for example, Leo Marx, *The Machine in the Garden: Technology and the Pastoral Ideal in America* (New York: Oxford University Press, 1964).
5. *Proceedings of the AFL-CIO 5th Constitutional Convention* (Washington, D.C.: American Federation of Labor–Congress of Industrial Organizations), p. 31.
6. Arthur Neef, "International Trends in Productivity and Unit Labor Costs in Manufacturing," *Monthly Labor Review* (December 1986).
7. U.S. Department of Labor, Bureau of Labor Statistics, *Handbook of Labor Statistics,* Bulletin 2175 (Washington, D.C.: Government Printing Office, December 1983), p. 247.
8. Harley Shaiken, Stephen Haerzenberg, and Sarah Kuhn, "The Work Process under More Flexible Production," *Industrial Relations* (Spring 1986).
9. Wikham Skinner, "Wanted: Managers for the Factory of the Future," in Robert J. Miller, (ed.) "Robotics: Future Factories, Future Workers," *Annals* (November 1983).
10. John R. Schermerhorn, Jr., *Management for Productivity,* 2d ed. (New York: Wiley, 1986), p. 191.

Chapter 1

1. For a fuller description, see chap. 3 of *Computerized Manufacturing Automation: Employment, Education, and the Workplace,* Report of the Office of Technology Assessment (Washington, D.C.: Government Printing Office, April 1984).
2. Ibid., p. 43.
3. "Automation and the Bottom Line," *Industry Week,* Maya 26, 1986.
4. "CAD/CAM: From Concept to Creation," *Business Month* (February 1984).
5. *Computerized Manufacturing Automation,* p. 57.
6. See David F. Noble, *Forces of Production* (New York: Alfred A. Knopf, 1984).

Chapter 2

1. Lawrence Schein, *Current Issues in Human-Resource Management,* Research Bulletin No. 190 (New York: Conference Board, 1986).

Chapter 4

1. Correlations between employee acceptance of change and perceived job security are reported in the literature. See, for example, F. Fox and B. Straw, "The Trapped Administrator: Effects of Job Security and Policy Resistance upon Commitment to a Course of Action," *Administrative Science Quarterly* 24, no. 3 (1979).

Chapter 5

1. See, for example, T.W. Schultz, "Investment in Human Capital," *American Economic Review* (March 1961): 1–17; and Gary S. Becker, *Human Capital* (New York: Columbia University Press, 1964).

Chapter 6

1. Pat Choate, *Retooling the American Work Force* (Washington, D.C.: Northeast-Midwest Institute, 1982, p. 2) citing a prediction in Peter F. Drucker, "The Next American Work Force: Demographics and U.S. Economic Policy," in *Economic Development Commentary* (Washington, D.C.: National Council for Urban Economic Development, October 1981).
2. *Hartford (Connecticut) Courant,* January 3, 1986.
3. See Nathan Rosenberg, *Technology and American Economic Growth* (Armonk, N.Y.: M.E. Sharpe, 1972).

Chapter 7

1. For an analysis of such practices, see, for example, Lee Dyer, Felician Foltman, and George Milkovich, "Contemporary Employment Stabilization Practices," in Thomas A. Kochan and Thomas A. Barocci, *Human Resource Management and Industrial Relations* (Boston: Little, Brown, 1985), pp. 203–214.
2. "IBM's Fancy Footwork to Sidestep Layoffs," *Business Week*, July 7, 1986, pp. 54–55.
3. Garth Mangum, Donald Mayall, and Kristin Nelson, "The Temporary Help Industry: A Response to the Dual Internal Labor Market," *Industrial and Labor Relations Review* (July 1985): 599–611.
4. See, for example, Bennett Harrison, *Education, Training and The Urban Ghetto* (Baltimore: Johns Hopkins Press, 1972), esp. chap. 5.
5. See, for example, John Kenneth Galbraith, *The New Industrial State* (Boston: Houghton Mifflin, 1967).
6. Mangum, Mayall, and Nelson, "The Temporary Help Industry."
7. Charles D. Spenser & Associates, as reported in *What's New in Collective Bargaining* (Washington, D.C.: Bureau of National Affairs, January 16, 1986).

Chapter 8

1. David A. Hounshell, *From the American System to Mass Production, 1800–1932* (Baltimore: Johns Hopkins Press, 1984), p. 120.
2. On this point, see Michael J. Piore and Charles F. Sabel, *The Second Industrial Divide* (New York: Basic Books, 1984).
3. Thomas A. Kochan and Thomas A. Barocci, *Human Resource Management and Industrial Relations* (Boston: Little, Brown, 1985), p. 396.
4. Gerald Nadler and Gordon H. Robinson, "Design for the Automated Factory: More Than Robots," *The Annals* (November 1983).
5. Larry Hirschhorn, *Beyond Mechanization: Work and Technology in a Postindustrial Age* (Cambridge, Mass.: MIT Press, 1986), p. 1.
6. Bill Sapor, "The Revolt against Working Smarter," *Fortune*, July 21, 1986.
7. On this issue, see Marvin E. Rozen, *The Economics of Work Organization* (New York: Praeger, 1983), esp. chap. 6.
8. Lester C. Thurow, *The Zero-Sum Solution: Building a World Class American Economy* (New York: Simon & Schuster, 1985), p. 186.
9. *Daily Labor Report*, November 14, 1986.

Chapter 9

1. JMA Research Institute, *Robotization: Its Implications for Management* (Tokyo: Fuji Corporation, 1983), pp. 69–73.
2. *New York Times*, December 2, 1986.
3. "New Technology: Manpower Aspects of the Management of Change,"

Report of a Study Group Visit to North America, Heavy Electrical Machinery EDC (London: National Economic Development Office, November 1984).

4. John Holuska, "Technology, a New Way to Build Cars," *New York Times,* March 13, 1986.

5. Harley Shaiken, "The Automated Factory: The View from the Shop Floor," *Technology Review* (January 1985).

6. Harley Shaiken, Stephen Haerzenberg, and Sarah Kuhn, "The Work Process under More Flexible Production," *Industrial Relations* (Spring 1986).

7. See, for example, E.L. Trist and K.W. Bamforth, "Some Social and Psychological Consequences of the Longwall Method of Coal-Getting," *Human Relations* (February 1951): 3–38. For a more fully developed view, see Eric Trist, *The Evolution of Socio-Technical Systems* (Toronto: Ontario Quality of Work Life Centre, 1981).

8. Denis D. Umsot, *Understanding Organizational Behavior* (St. Paul, Minn.: West Publishing, 1984), p. 160.

9. J. Richard Hackman, "Work Design," in J. Richard Hackman and J. Lloyd Settle, (eds.), *Improving Life at Work* (Santa Monica, Calif.: Goodyear Publishing, 1977), pp. 111–115.

10. Amil Verma and Thomas A. Kochan, "The Growth and Nature of the Nonunion Sector within a Firm," in Thomas A. Kochan, ed., *Challenges and Choices Facing American Labor* (Cambridge, Mass.: MIT Press, 1985), p. 113.

11. Thomas A. Kochan, Harry C. Katz, and Nancy R. Mower, *Worker Participation and American Unions: Threat or Opportunity?* (Kalamazoo, Mich.: W.E. Upjohn Institute for Employment Research, 1984), pp. 84–96. They also report a case of failure of a sociotechnical system at a new Ontario meat-cutting plant, attributable mainly to the resentment of the skilled butchers toward job rotation and loss of authority and status.

Chapter 10

1. CAD/CAM: "From Concept to Creation," *Business Month* (February 1984).

2. Rita R. Schreiber, "Changing the Mind-set in Robotics," *Robotics Today* (February 1986).

3. John Teresco, "Planning for the Factory of the Future," *Industry Week,* January 10, 1985.

4. *New York Times,* January 6, 1986.

5. Ibid., September 4, 1986.

6. Wickham Skinner, "Wanted: Managers for the Factory of the Future," *The Annals* (November 1983).

7. Sara Kiesler, "New Technology in the Work Place," *Public Relations Journal* (December 1983).

8. See Tom Burns and G.M. Stalker, *The Management of Innovation* (London: Tavistock Publications, 1961), pp. 119–125.

9. John R. Schermerhorn, Jr., *Management for Productivity,* 2d ed. (New York: Wiley, 1986), p. 191. © 1986. Reprinted with permission.

Chapter 11

1. Richard N. Block and Kenneth McLennan, "Structural Economic Change and Industrial Relations in the United States' Manufacturing and Transportation Sectors since 1973," in Hervey Juris, Mark Thompson, and Wilbur Daniels, eds., *Industrial Relltions in a Decade of Economic Change* (Madison, Wisc.: Industrial Relations Research Association, 1985), p. 345.
2. "New Technology," *The Machinist* (September 1984): 15.
3. Bill Sapor, "The Revolt against Working Smarter," *Fortune*, July 21, 1986.
4. Larry Hirschhorn, *Beyond Mechanization: Work and Technology in a Post-industrial Age* (Cambridge, Mass.: MIT Press, 1986), p. 140.
5. Fred K. Foulkes, "Large Nonunionized Employers," in Jack Steiber, Robert B. McKersie, and D. Quinn Mills, eds., *U.S. Industrial Relations 1950–1980: A Critical Assessment* (Madison, Wisc.: Industrial Relations Research Association, 1981), p. 151.

Chapter 12

1. See, for example, Jerome A. Mark, "Technological Change and Employment: Some Results from BLS Research," *Monthly Labor Review* (April 1987).
2. *Monthly Labor Review* (September 1987).
3. *Daily Labor Report*, August 1, 1984, pp. E2, E3.

Index

Accident rates, 75–76
Accounting systems, robots and, 3
Aerospace electronics manufacturer, union response and, 105
Age: employee response and, 26, 27; employment and, 49–50; retraining and, 33, 36
Aircraft instrumentation manufacturer: computer testing and, 70; employment and, 48, 52
Aircraft plant: AMHS at, 4–5; technology introduction and, 11
AMHS. *See* Automated materials-handling systems
Anxiety, among employees, 17, 25
Appliance plant: communications in, 19–20; job broadening and, 73; nonsynchronous assembly line in, 69–70; technology introduction and, 12, 16; union response at, 105–106, 111
Apprentice schools, 41–42
Arbitration, of bargaining unit work disputes, 110
ASRS. *See* Automated storage and retrieval systems
Assembly work: nature of jobs and, 67–68; nonsynchronous line and, 69–70; robots in, 2
Attitudes: communications and, 20; of management toward employee involvement, 81, 83–84; technology introduction and, 16; of union toward employee involvement, 13, 81–83, 89, 116–119
Attrition, avoidance of displacement and, 57–59, 127
Authoritarianism, decline of, 84–85
Automated guided vehicles, 85–86
Automated materials-handling systems (AMHS), 4–5
Automated storage and retrieval systems (ASRS), 5; communications and, 18; safety and, 75
Automobile plant: employee involvement at, 82–83; employment and, 49; robots in, 2; union response at, 108, 109–110, 118
Automotive components manufacturer, union response and, 105

Bargaining unit work, 109–111
Bearing plant: CNC at, 4; employment and, 46
Blue-collar jobs, disappearance of, 50
Buffers, avoiding displacement and, 58

Cable manufacturing plant: employee involvement at, 88; technology introduction at, 14
CAD. *See* Computer-aided design
CAD/CAM, interdepartmental cooperation and, 93–95
CAM Systems Engineering, 94
Capital investment, 54
Chemical company: implementation of programmable automation at, 8; technology introduction at, 11, 14
CIM. *See* Computer-integrated manufacturing
Cleanliness, 76
CNC. *See* Computerized numerical control machines
Collective bargaining, communications and, 21–23. *See also* Union(s); Union response
Communication(s), 17–23, 128, 134; collective bargaining requirements and, 21–23; company efforts and, 17–18; forms of, 18–19; inadequate, 21; industrial relations climate and, 19–20
Communications equipment manufacturer, employment and, 45–46, 48–49

Compensation: as benefit for displaced workers, 65–66; employee involvement and, 88; intraplant transfers and, 62–63; unions and, 111–113
Competition: employment and, 44–47; foreign, 44–47, 134
Computer-aided design (CAD), 1–2
Computer-aided engineering, 2
Computer-controlled systems, 6
Computer-integrated manufacturing (CIM), 6; interdepartmental cooperation and, 93–95
Computerized numerical control machines (CNC), 3–4; seniority and, 105
Computer manufacturer: implementation of programmable automation at, 8; technology introduction and, 11–12
Computer monitoring, of work performance, 76–77, 104
Computer testing, 70
Cooperation, interdepartmental, 93
Cost reduction, job broadening and, 73
Counseling, displacement and, 131

Decision making, downward movement of, 69, 134
Defense contractors, employment and, 48
Departmental organization, 93–95
Design, for automation, 54, 94
Deskilling, 70–72
Digital Equipment Corporation, 95
Displacement, 11–12, 57–66; attrition and, 57–59, 127; benefits for displaced workers and, 65–66; counseling and, 131; early retirement and, 27, 60–61, 116; employee reassignment and, 65; interplant transfers and, 63–65, 115; intraplant transfers and, 62–63, 114–115; temporary employees and, 59–60
Diversified products manufacturer, union response and, 122
Dollar, employment and, 44
Dual labor market, 59–60

Early retirement, 60–61, 116; employee response and, 27

Economic factors, 55, 134, employment and, 44; growth and, 54, 131
Economic security, unions and, 113–116
Educational institutions, role in training, 40–42, 133
Efficiency, employment and, 54
Electrical components plant: ASRS at, 5; employment and, 47, 51–52; implementation of programmable automation at, 7
Electronic control device manufacturer: employment and, 45, 51; job broadening and, 73
Electronics plant: ASRS at, 5; CNC at, 4; job broadening and, 74; union response and, 108
Employee(s): anxiety among, 17, 25; assistance to, 19; matching with jobs, 33–34; reassignment of, 65; recognition and, 26; reluctance to relocate, 64; responses of, 25–29; temporary, 59–60
Employee involvement, 77, 79–91; contrasting views of, 86; development of, 79–81; management attitudes toward, 81, 83–84; sociotechnical approaches to, 14–16, 27, 79, 86–88, 118; technology and, 84–86; technology introduction and, 13; training for, 88–91, 127; unions and, 13, 81–83, 89, 116–119
Employee placement center, 65
Employee relations: technology introduction and, 9–13. See also Labor-management relations
Employment, 43–55; complexity of problems and, 43–47; increase in, 48–49; labor force composition and, 50–53; positive role of innovation and, 47–48; short-term outlook for, 54–55; women, minorities, and young workers and, 49–50
Engineers, retraining and, 36–37
Environmental controls company, union response at, 114
Ephlin, Donald, 82
Equal employment laws, 49

Flexible automation, 4

Foreign competition, 134; employment and, 44–47

Gain sharing, 112–113
General Electric, 118; robots and, 3
General Motors, 71, 79, 85–86, 87, 95
Gold plating, automation of line for, 74
Government: income maintenance programs and, 132–133; role in training and relocation, 130–131, 132
Grievances, 116; in nonunion plants, 120
Group leader approach, 82

Human relations training, 38, 127
Human resource planning, 9–13, 135; importance of, 125, 126–127

IBM, 58
Improshare plan, 113
Incentive systems, 112–113
Income extension aid, 65–66
Income maintenance programs, 66, 132–133
Industrial robots. See Robots
Industry-university cooperation, training and, 40–42, 133
In-house training, vendors versus, 39–40
Instrument manufacturing company, technology introduction at, 12
Interdepartmental cooperation, 93
Interplant transfers, 63–65, 115
Intraplant transfers, avoiding displacement and, 62–63, 114–115
Inventory, implementation of programmable automation and, 7

Japan: employee involvement in, 79; management approach in, 133; training in, 31
Job(s): blue-collar, disappearance of, 50; broadening, 32, 72–74, 107–109; changing nature of, 67–70; expansion of, 69; matching workers with, 33–34
Job classifications: employee response and, 28; intraplant transfers and, 114–115; reduction in, 70–71; unions and, 107–109
Job displacement. See Displacement

Job enlargement, upskilling through, 70
Job placement, 65, 66, 131
Job guarantees, 58
Job interest, employee response and, 25–26
Job rotation, 87
Job security, 126; employee response and, 25; unions and, 113–116

Labor costs, employment and, 45
Labor force: composition of, 50–53; tendency of women to leave, 61
Labor-management committees, in-plant, 122–123
Labor-management relations, 103–104, 122–123, 127–128; communications and, 19–20, 21; nonunion, 119–121. See also Union(s); Union response
Labor market, dual, 59–60. See also employment
Length of service, employee response and, 27
Living standards, changing nature of work and, 68

Maintenance, job broadening and, 72–73, 107–108
Maintenance workers, retraining and, 34–35
Management: attitudes toward employee involvement, 81, 83–84; new styles of, 95–97; retraining and, 37–38. See also Labor-management relations
Managerial-supervisory group: attitudes toward employee involvement, 83–84, 90; impact on, 96; resistance of, 28, 120, 125; retraining and, 35–36
Manufacturing automation protocol (MAP), 95
Market demand, employment and, 44–48
Mass production, nature of jobs and, 67–68
Mechanistic structure, 98
Metalworking industries, employee involvement in, 86
Mexican-Americans, employment and, 49

Minorities, employment and, 49–50
Motivation, to increase knowledge and versatility, 77
Motivational systems, 69

National Committee on Technological Progress, 22–23
NC. *See* Numerical control machines
NCM. *See* Numerical control machinist
No-layoff policy, 58
Nonsynchronous assembly line, 69–70
Nuclear materials: safety and, 14, 74
Numerical control machines (NC), 3–4
Numerical control machinist (NCM), 105

Office equipment manufacturer: communications and, 17; technology introduction and, 15; union response and, 108, 114, 117
Open organization, 97–98
Organic structure, 98
Outplacement, 65, 66, 131

Peer training, 40
Performance, computer monitoring of, 76–77, 104
Performance ratings, interdepartmental cooperation and, 93
Personnel, continuity of, 14. *See also* Employee(s); Management; Managerial supervisory group
Placement center, 65
Plant cleanliness, 76
Plant departmental organization, 93–95
Product design, 54, 94
Production workers: impact on, 51; retraining of, 34–35
Productivity growth, 129–130
Product market demand, employment and, 44–48
Programmable automation, implementation of, 6–8
Programming, responsibility for, 71–72
Public policy, 129

Quality circles, 79, 84
Quality control: implementation of programmable automation and, 7; vision systems and, 6
Quality of work life (QWL) approach, 80, 117–118, 119; union response to, 81–83, 116
Quality teams, social isolation and, 77
QWL. *See* Quality of work life approach

Railroad equipment manufacturer: employment and, 47–48; union response and, 105
Rate protection, intraplant transfers and, 63
Recognition, employee response and, 26
"Red circle rates," intraplant transfers and, 63
Relocation, government's role in, 132
Retirement, early. *See* Early retirement
Retraining. *See* Training
Return-on-investment (ROI), robots and, 3
Reward systems, 69. *See also* Compensation
Robot(s), 2–3; accident rates and, 75–76; applications of, 2; limitations of, 2–3
Robotics Institute of America, 2
Rucker plan, 112–113

Sabotage, 120
Safety, 74–76
Scanlon plan, 112–113
Scientific management, 67–68
Self-contained modules, 93
Seniority: employment and, 50; interplant transfer and, 115; retraining and, 34; unions and, 104–107
Setup: job broadening and, 70, 73
Severance pay, 65
Shipyard, employee involvement at, 84
Singer Sewing Machine Company, 67
Skill(s): employee response and, 25; need for, 130
Skill mix, changing, 73–74
Skill twist, 53
Social isolation, 77
Society, impact of change on, 129
Sociotechnical approach, 14–16, 79, 86–91, 118; employee response and, 27; training for, 88–91

Special-purpose machinery, 68
Steel plant: computerized control system at, 6; employee involvement at, 88, 89, 91; employment at, 46–47; labor-management conflict at, 104; union response at, 106–107, 110, 119
Suggestion system, 14
Supervisors. *See* Managerial-supervisory group
Supplementary unemployment benefits, 65–66
Synthetics plant: ASRS at, 5; computerized control system at, 6; employee involvement at, 87–88

Tandon Corp., 58
Tavistock Institute, 86
Taylor, Frederick W., 67–68
Team approach, 14–16; autonomous, 91; social isolation and, 77. *See also* Quality of work life approach; Sociotechnical approach
Technological change, pace of, 26
Technology, employee response and, 25
Technology introduction, 9–16; employee involvement in, 13–16; role of employee relations in, 9–13
Telecommunications manufacturer: communications at, 17, 22; technology introduction at, 10–11; union response at, 113
Temporary employees, avoiding displacement and, 59–60
Time, robots and, 3
Toyota, 79
Training, 31–42, 53, 127; apprentice schools and, 41–42; designing programs for, 38–42; employee involvement and, 88; of engineers, 36–37; government's role in, 130–131, 132; industry-university cooperation and, 40–42, 133; intraplant transfers and, 62; of management, 37–38; matching jobs and workers and, 33–34; need for, 31–33; peer, 40; of production and maintenance workers, 34–35; programming and, 71; recommendations for, 42; for sociotechnical approach, 88–91; of supervisors and other salaried personnel, 35–36
Transfers, 126, 127; interplant, 63–65, 115; intraplant, 62–63, 114–115
Transportation equipment components manufacturer, communications and, 21

UAW. *See* United Auto Workers
Unemployment benefits, supplementary, 65–66
Union(s): communications and, 17–18, 19–20, 21–23; coordination of, interplant transfer and, 115; decline in strength of, 101; employee response and, 27; employment and, 46; interplant transfers and, 63–64; intraplant transfers and, 62; jurisdictional disputes among, 111; technology introduction and, 12–13. *See also* Labor-management relations
Union responses, 101–123; bargaining unit work and, 109–111; compensation and, 111–113; economic security and, 113–116; employee involvement and, 13, 81–83, 89, 116–119; job classifications and, 107–109; labor-management conflict and, 103–104; national versus local, 102–103; seniority and, 104–107
United Auto Workers (UAW), 71, 82, 87
United States, world economy and, 44–47, 55, 134
Universities, role in training, 40–42, 133
Upskilling, 52–53, 70–72

Vendors, in-house training versus, 39–40
Vision systems, 5–6
Volvo, 87

Women: employment and, 49–50; tendency to leave labor force, 61
Work cells, 84
Work environment, 74–76
Work flow, employee response and, 27–28
Work groups, 18–19; autonomous,

87; foremanless, 82. *See also* Quality of work life approach; Sociotechnical approach; Team approach
Work performance, computer monitoring of, 76–77, 104
Work rule changes, communications and, 21

Work simplification, 68
World economy, 134; United States and, 55

Young workers, employment and, 49–50

About the Author

Roy B. Helfgott is Distinguished Professor of Economics at the New Jersey Institute of Technology, as well as being a member of the Graduate Faculty, Rutgers University. In addition to IRC, Dr. Helfgott has conducted economic research and analysis for Organization Resources Counselors, Inc., the United Nations, the New York Metropolitan Region Study, and the International Ladies Garment Workers' Union. He was a Senior Fulbright Research Scholar in the United Kingdom, and has taught at Baruch College and the Pennsylvania State University.

Dr. Helfgott received a B.S. degree from City College, New York, an M.A. from Columbia University, and a Ph.D. from the New School for Social Research. He is coauthor of *Management, Automation, and People* (IRC, 1964), *Industrial Planning* (United Nations, 1969), and *Made in New York: Case Studies in Metropolitan Manufacturing* (Harvard, 1959), and author of *Labor Economics* (Random House, 1974, 1980), as well as numerous other publications.